Praise for *Stray Dogs, Saints, and Saviors*

"Russo's observation of Locke's transformation by Green Dot shows that education reform is complex, hard work that can't be done with a quick fix. Russo weaves together fascinating anecdotes and lively descriptions of the people and events that helped turned Locke from a failing school to one of hope and survival. While I don't agree with what's said about the United Teachers of Los Angeles, *Stray Dogs, Saints, and Saviors* is an important addition to the collection of books about making sustainable improvement in our public schools."

—Randi Weingarten, president,
American Federation of Teachers

"For once, in Alexander Russo's talented hands, school reform is not boring. His book has drama, tension, danger, heartbreak and joy—all played out in what was once one of the worst high schools in America. It will be impossible for you to put it down."
—Jay Mathews, *Washington Post* education columnist
and author, *Work Hard. Be Nice*

"Part scholar, part journalist, part urban wayfarer, Alexander Russo aims a bright, unflinching light at the transformation of one of America's most troubled high schools. He writes with nuance and honesty and—in spite of all the complexities and contradictions—hope."
—Jesse Katz, Pulitzer-prize winning journalist and author,
The Opposite Field

"*Stray Dogs, Saints, and Saviors* offers an important, up-close glimpse into school reform's promise and perils. Alexander Russo threads the needle between healthy appreciation for Green Dot's impact on improving kids' lives and hard-nosed skepticism about the 'new' Locke's impact."
—Greg Toppo, education reporter for *USA Today*
and Spencer Education Journalism Fellow

"As public school systems shift their attention to turning-around the nation's lowest-performing schools, the story of Locke High School is undoubtedly going to serve as a guide of sorts. Alexander Russo gets at the real story—not the feel-good, made-for-television version—and in the process gives us all a solid baseline upon which we can assess the long-term success or failure of Green Dot's ambitious school turn-around effort. In education reform's push to make things black and white, Russo shows that the real action is in the gray area."

—Joe Williams, executive director, Democrats for Education Reform and author, *Cheating Our Kids: How Politics and Greed Ruin Education*

"A gripping tale of challenge, hope, disappointment, success, scandal and persistence in the school-reform maze, penned by a deft and knowledgeable writer."

—Chester E. Finn Jr., senior fellow, Hoover Institution, Stanford University and president, Thomas B. Fordham Institute

"Alexander Russo has penned a remarkable account of one of the decade's most intriguing school reform efforts. Delightfully, his narrative manages to do justice to the exploits of colorful Green Dot founder Steve Barr, the outsized icon behind the audacious takeover of L.A.'s Locke High School. This is a must-read for educators, policymakers, and parents who wonder what can be done about troubled urban schools."

—Frederick M. Hess, director of education policy studies, American Enterprise Institute and author, *The Same Thing Over and Over*

"Like all great social movements in American history, school reform is a story not just of airy principles but of gritty struggles on the ground—of stops and starts, frustrating obstacles and unsatisfying compromise, flesh and blood in the battle to rescue the next generation. Alexander Russo brings it all alive in one high school trying to come back from the dead. This is a compelling view of the most critical domestic issue of our time."

—Jonathan Alter, author, *The Promise: President Obama, Year One*

"At a time when the debate on education reform has sunk to finger-pointing and scapegoating, Alexander Russo has provided a welcome corrective. He refuses to give us cartoon villains or saintly heroes. Instead he takes us indelibly and memorably into the struggle to remake a failing school. There's optimism in this book, but it's the measured optimism that comes from keen observation and independent thinking."

—Samuel G. Freedman, professor,
Graduate School of Journalism, Columbia University
and author, *Small Victories: The Real World of a Teacher*

"An insightful and eye-opening analysis of the effort to turnaround Alain Leroy Locke High School; one of America's most troubled schools. Russo is a great story teller who presents his readers with a vivid and detailed description of the complex issues confronting the school and those who attempt to reform it. *Stray Dogs* is a 'must read' for those interested in understanding what it will take to reform urban schools."

—Pedro Noguera, Peter L. Agnew Professor
of Education, New York University
and author, *The Trouble with Black Boys*

"Russo's *Stray Dogs* is a deep-dive into the world of public schools. With tenacity and compassion, Russo brings us into the complicated world of public education, where the stakes are high and the expectations great. Rarely have we been given such a close-up look into the day-to-day struggles of teachers, students, and administrators. One comes away with an appreciation of how hard it is to teach, and to do it right every day."

—Sudhir Venkatesh, William B. Ransford Professor
of Sociology, Columbia University and author,
Gang Leader for a Day

"An important tale of how a troubled school can be changed and the children who thrive—or not—as a result of thoughtful reform. Russo gets past piety and politics and gives us a valuable look at the people who try, fail and try again to help kids succeed in education."

—Peg Tyre, author, *New York Times* best-selling book
The Trouble With Boys

"Alexander Russo takes us deep inside a tough urban high school. His book, *Stray Dogs, Saints and Saviors*, demonstrates in lively prose that Green Dot is a lot more than Steve Barr. This is a fast read and a gripping story."

—John Merrow, education correspondent,
PBS NewsHour and author, *Below C Level*

"Writing in a style that combines good investigative reporting with good ethnography, Alexander Russo has produced a powerfully instructive book on a powerfully important topic. The message is that school turnarounds could be a powerful instrument for good, but only if we see through the hype. In vivid detail, Russo demonstrates that it is possible for a dysfunctional school to get better, but the time, money, hard work and smart politicking required are an order of magnitude beyond what many pundits believe."

—Charles Payne, the Frank P. Hixon Distinguished Service
Professor in the School of Social Service
Administration, University of Chicago and author,
So Much Reform, So Little Change

STRAY DOGS, SAINTS, AND SAVIORS

To my mother, Jeremy Warburg Russo,
for the love and support she has always provided;
and to my father, William Russo,
for the warmth and creativity he embodied

STRAY DOGS, SAINTS, AND SAVIORS

Fighting for the Soul
of America's Toughest High School

ALEXANDER RUSSO

JOSSEY-BASS
A Wiley Imprint
www.josseybass.com

Published by Jossey-Bass
A Wiley Imprint
989 Market Street, San Francisco, CA 94103-1741—www.josseybass.com

Illustration of Locke High School by David Leonard.

Readers should be aware that Internet Web sites offered as citations and/or sources for further information may have changed or disappeared between the time this was written and when it is read.

Jossey-Bass books and products are available through most bookstores. To contact Jossey-Bass directly call our Customer Care Department within the U.S. at 800-956-7739, outside the U.S. at 317-572-3986, or fax 317-572-4002.

Jossey-Bass also publishes its books in a variety of electronic formats. Some content that appears in print may not be available in electronic books.

Library of Congress Cataloging-in-Publication Data has been applied for.

ISBN 978-1-118-00175-2 (hardcover); 978-1-118-03357-9 (ebk.); 978-1-118-03358-6 (ebk.); 978-1-118-03359-3 (ebk.)

Printed in the United States of America
FIRST EDITION
HB Printing   10 9 8 7 6 5 4 3 2 1

Contents

PART THREE   Becoming a School

Acknowledgments

It goes without saying that this book would not have been possible without the participation and candor of everyone at Green Dot and at Locke High School, including both those whose roles are described prominently in the book and many others whose role in helping the turnaround effort deserves more attention than it receives here. This includes dean of students Mike Moody; English teachers Maggie Callender, Kevin Sully, Keith Kobylka, Monica Stone, and Joshua Berardall; math teachers Fernando Avila, Stephanie Avila, and Peggy Gorsich; campus aide and coach Vic Lopez; science teacher Dennis Stein; Green Dot Education Chief Cristina de Jesus; and many, many others. All deserve credit for sharing their stories for the larger good.

I thank Kate Gagnon, Tracy Gallagher, Lesley Iura, Pamela Berkman, Michele Jones, and everyone else at Jossey-Bass for their interest and support. It's not easy helping an irascible forty-six-year-old rookie through the book-writing process. I appreciate their assistance and patience at every step of the way. David Lobenstine provided incredibly helpful editing during the development stages. Paula Breen was a great help vetting the legal issues and guiding me through contract negotiations. Maya Stanton was an indefatigable fact checker.

This book would not have been possible without the generous assistance of everyone involved with the Spencer Education

Journalism Fellowship at Columbia University's Graduate School of Journalism, including most notably the Spencer Foundation's Paul Goren and Mike McPherson and Columbia's Arlene Morgan, LynNell Hancock, Sam Freedman, Jeff Henig, Paula Span, Kevin Coyne, and Nick Lemann. Special thanks to my 2008–2009 Spencer "classmates," Nancy Solomon and Claudia Wallis.

There are several colleagues, mentors, and betters who have helped me with advice, encouragement, and criticism at key moments during the lengthy process. These include Stephanie Banchero, Greg Toppo, Roland Lange, Peg Tyre, Susan Wallace, John Ayers, Virginia Vitzthum, Jay Mathews, Joel Rubin, Joe Williams, Jonathan Gyurko, Edward Lewine, Amanda Millner-Fairbanks, Stacey Schultz, Donna Foote, Peter Green, John Merrow, Jacob Weisberg, Paul Glastris, and David Zivan. Like they say, I couldn't have done it without you.

I also express my sincere thanks to colleagues and publications that have supported my work along the way, including Scholastic Administrator (which sponsors my national education blog, This Week in Education) and ChicagoNow (which sponsors District 299, my Chicago schools blog), as well as *Catalyst Chicago*'s Linda Lenz, *EdWeek*'s Virginia Edwards and Jeanne McCann, AASA's Jay Goldman and the *Title I Report*'s Julie Miller. I appreciate all the collegiality, encouragement, and support over the years—especially the early ones.

Character List

Reggie Andrews: The veteran music teacher (and cowriter of "Let It Whip") is "more Locke" than almost anyone else and regards outside do-gooders with understandable wariness.

Steve Barr: A latecomer to school reform, the irascible Barr starts a much-publicized network of Los Angeles charter schools but knows that charter schools and newsclips aren't enough.

Veronica ("Ronnie") Coleman: The forty-something rookie principal from Michigan initially doesn't want the job running the biggest program at Locke—and some community members don't want her to have the spot either.

Zeus "Hollywood" Cubias: A math teacher who graduated from Locke in 1992, the glib El Salvadoran becomes the public face of the "new" Locke despite his ambivalence about "the Dot."

David: The good-looking senior used to get good grades but now spends so much time in trouble that he's become a major source of disagreement among the administrators in charge of his fate, each of whom have tried and failed to help him.

Emily Kaplowitz: Guidance counselor extraordinaire, "Miss K" is instrumental in helping get the new school organized and keeping it afloat, but sometimes advocates for students so hard that she runs into conflicts with colleagues.

CHARACTER LIST

Monica Mayall: New to Locke but one of the most experienced teachers at the new school, the veteran art and drama teacher is dismayed at Green Dot's lapses and becomes the union rep for the school.

Mike Moody: The well-dressed, stern-faced former Division I football player is in charge of working with misbehaving students but is trying to do so without harsh disciplinary measures. Cubias calls him "Reverend" for his snazzy dress and fastidious, churchgoing ways.

Lieutenant Alex Moore: The heavyset security guard is in charge of keeping the school and surrounding streets safe for kids and teachers, but not everyone is confident that the "LT" is up to the job (or happy having armed guards posted all around the campus).

Marco Petruzzi: The slender, Italian-born Petruzzi spent fifteen years as an international business consultant and left a partnership at Bain & Company to join Green Dot, eventually becoming Barr's successor as CEO.

Ricky: Smart, mistrustful and angry at kids and adults alike, Ricky is one of the many kids who gets caught up in the violence that overwhelms the school one sunny day at the end of lunch and has to figure out if he can abide by all the new rules and regulations long enough to graduate.

Bruce Smith: The cerebral English teacher is one of the first to see the advantages of bringing Green Dot into Locke and ends up being instrumental in making that a reality, but what role, if any, he'll have with Green Dot is uncertain.

Frank Wells: Appointed to take over Locke in 2004, the soft-spoken principal is the catalyst for the turnaround of Locke and hopes to help Green Dot revive the school.

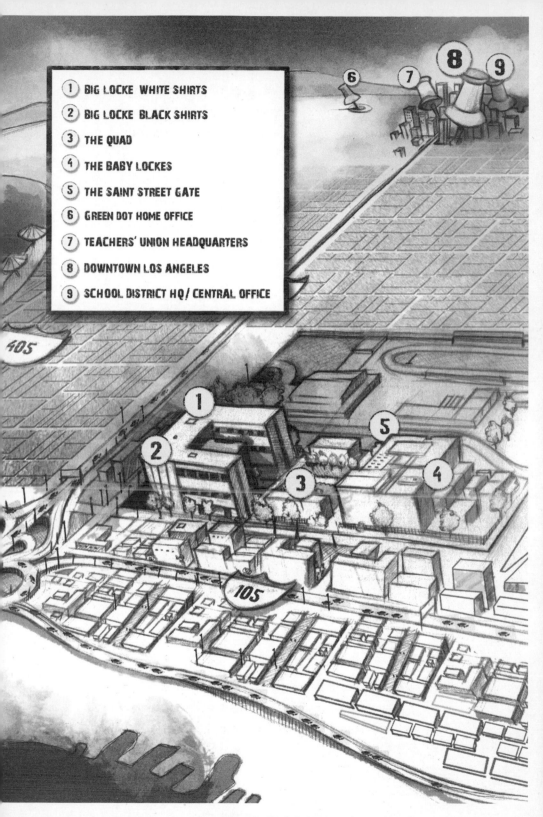

1. BIG LOCKE WHITE SHIRTS
2. BIG LOCKE BLACK SHIRTS
3. THE QUAD
4. THE BABY LOCKES
5. THE SAINT STREET GATE
6. GREEN DOT HOME OFFICE
7. TEACHERS' UNION HEADQUARTERS
8. DOWNTOWN LOS ANGELES
9. SCHOOL DISTRICT HQ / CENTRAL OFFICE

Map of Locke High School

Introduction

It was just a month after the massive May 2008 brawl that shut down Alain Leroy Locke High School and made national news that I first visited the sprawling Watts campus, heading down the 110 Freeway to meet school reformer Steve Barr and tour the hallways. The light-blue paint on the outside walls was faded and patched. A twenty-five-foot-high fence surrounded the campus, looking like something you'd see in a prison or at a border crossing rather than a school. The burned-out press box above the football field resembled a guard tower. A big blue wall had been erected along the east side of campus in the wake of a student's shooting death. And yet, the place didn't feel particularly dangerous.

Waved in through the front gate by a yellow-jacketed campus aide, Barr and I strolled the near-empty halls and sunny walkways, chatting about the process that—nearly a year before—had culminated in Locke teachers voting to hand the school over to Barr's nonprofit charter school organization, Green Dot Public Schools. As usual, Barr was dressed casually, wearing an untucked polo shirt a baseball cap pulled low over his blue eyes.

Even before the campuswide melee that brought riot police and TV helicopters to the campus, it had been an awful year for Locke and a difficult transition for Green Dot. "We did this thing entirely ass-backwards," said Barr, standing near the gate where much of the fighting had taken place. Now, three weeks before graduation, the low-slung buildings already had a sleepy, off-season feeling to them. Hundreds of students had dropped out during the course of the year, and many more had been told not to come back after the violence. Graffiti "tags" were everywhere—as were pasty-looking district administrators sent out from their cubicles to patrol the campus for the rest of the year and prevent any repeat fighting. All of the neglect and lethargy were supposed to change on July 1, when the school district officially handed the campus and all it contained over to Green Dot, and the education world watched to see if Barr's promise of a dramatically better education for the kids of Watts panned out.

My coming to Locke that day was the culmination of a series of events begun nearly twenty years ago, in the very early 1990s, when as a twenty-something education wonk working in Washington DC, I gradually came to appreciate that the divide between teachers unions and school administrators and charter school advocates was in many ways as deep and entrenched as any partisan divide between Democrats and Republicans. At the beginning of my career, I had assumed that everyone was, generally, on the same side: all Democrats, all focused on education. (This was before Republicans were prominent in education issues, or so it seemed). I interviewed for jobs with union presidents as well as school district administrators, with centrist Democrats and with liberals. But slowly I realized that teachers unions and charter school advocates rarely coexisted peacefully, and that teachers unions and school districts were in many places constantly battling, the Hatfields and McCoys of the education world. Like many, I was ambivalent about this long-running trench warfare going on between them (and their shared enemy, charter schools), all the stalemated finger pointing and speechifying and disjointed efforts. But then in 2007 I started hearing about something that seemed new—a unionized network of charter schools called Green Dot, and its founder Steve Barr's unlikely interest in fixing a broken district high school. The school would be converted from a traditional district school into a charter school, but the teachers would still be unionized, and the school would still serve all the kids in the neighborhood. Charter education, unionization, and full-size neighborhood high schools were a rare combination—a rainbow-colored unicorn in the forest. I applied for a Spencer Fellowship in education journalism—a paid year at Columbia University's journalism school—and decided to follow the story of Green Dot's attempt to "fix" Locke High School and share the story of what it's really like to try to do such an unusual and intriguing thing. This book is the result of those efforts.

The "new" Locke opened in September 2008, and it was a pretty exciting thing to see happen—the education version of an Internet start-up or a new Broadway show. Each morning, teachers, office workers, and administrators got to the school in the cool early morning hours to prepare for the start of the day. Then at 8:00 A.M. the kids streamed into the building through the gates and into the classrooms, and the daily performance began. Behind the scenes, office staff and administrators worked to handle any missed cues—missing teachers, after-school events, fights. The kids departed at the end of the day. Then it was time to get ready to do it again. Pretty much everybody was hoping for the best. From Hollywood to the *New York Times*, unlikely successes have always been a favorite. We all want to believe that transformation is possible; that dire, stubborn situations—be they academic or financial, economic or environmental—can turn dramatically, unexpectedly better, at least some of the time. The possibility of change, after all, is a deep-rooted American narrative. And so everyone wanted to believe that Locke could happen. I wasn't any different, a writer looking for a story to tell. I was just there longer than any other outsider.

But were we expecting too much? For years now it's been noted that American students are wildly overconfident—that too many seem to think that they're going to be professional athletes or performers or models or billionaires. It's an easy thing to tut-tut at these fantasies of glory, given how obviously unrealistic they are. But many of us adults hold our own equally unrealistic fantasies, which are arguably just as destructive as those of kids thinking they're going to be pro ball players. To me the most destructive of all is the expectation that any single person or idea or program can truly fix things for kids, save them reliably and completely. This belief—this adult version of kids' pro basketball player dreams—is entrenched in popular culture, in the news media, and in school reform circles, usually in the form of "magic bullet" and "secret sauce" stories focused on some special innovation that's being tried here and there, or "hero" stories in which an individual teacher, principal, reformer, or politician rides to the rescue. I'm not saying that these things haven't occasionally happened or aren't worth lauding and attempting to replicate, or that partial successes shouldn't be admired. But it seems to me that we should all be a little more grown up when we go into anything as difficult as improving schools, that any such efforts should be navigated with full knowledge of the complex, entrenched dynamics that have created the original situation and will challenge any changes. Any occasional successes, minor or miraculous, should be treated as a combination of luck, smarts, and effort that might just as well have failed, or may well falter next month or next year. But that's not how the results are usually played out, in the media or among reformers. Exceptions somehow become expectations, and then the cycle of disappointment and cynicism grows ever deeper.

The Locke turnaround story was no different. What I found over the two years that followed my first visit was that there were two different stories taking place. The story told in public followed a satisfying narrative of rescue and rebirth, exaggerating both the problems of the "old" Locke and the successes of the new school. Even before the first year was over, journalists and politicians had already declared it a success, a national model. This wasn't the first time that the media had prematurely glommed onto a promising story, but it was a particularly compact example. And then, just as quickly, the Locke turnaround was belittled as being incomplete (and expensive), and Green Dot's reputation was marred by internal convulsions despite the reality that the good work on the ground was partial. The teachers and students at Locke lived in their own, almost completely different world in which improvements were slower, less complete, more incre-mental than anything described publicly; setbacks were frequent and stubborn, and the relationship between the school and the Green Dot home office was sometimes as strained as any tra-ditional school dealing with a central office. This was a much more complicated, uncertain world, but it suffered little from the boom-and-bust narrative going on in the press and among reformers.

Somewhere in between the exaggerated spin cycle and the daily classroom grind was the true story of Locke, where things were slowly but steadily getting better thanks to the hard work and courage of teachers and administrators who spent every day with the kids and did everything they could think of to help them stay in school, pass their classes, graduate, and maybe even go on to college. Hence the title of this book: *Stray Dogs, Saints, and Saviors*. The stray dogs are the mutts that sometimes wandered in from the streets onto campus and into the quad even after the school had been revamped and the quad beautified with trees and grass. They are the poverty and neglect that Watts has endured for much too long. The saints—Locke's mascot—are the Locke community, past and present, which has pressed onward even when everyone else has forgotten it. The saviors are those teachers and leaders past and present who have tried to make things better—and put themselves through the wringer in the process.

Now well into its third year, the Locke transformation effort tells us that with tremendously hard work and sacrifice, a broken school can indeed be improved in meaningful ways. But the realities of change—halting and incremental, mostly frustrating and occasionally inspiring—don't match the desire of funders, policymakers, and the rest of us for simple, speedy success stories. The process of school reform is one of the most vital and least glamorous efforts in education, the unwanted job. The gap between uncertain reality and the smooth public narrative ultimately dooms our efforts at school improvement and chews up those flawed but dedicated individuals who make fixing schools their life's work.

A word about access and individuals' names: Though at times they regretted doing so, pretty much everyone at Green Dot gave me nearly complete access to the school and all its inner workings. My only promise was to be fair and to tell the truth. Names of students have been changed to protect their privacy during a particularly vulnerable time of life. Names of additional characters have been omitted in order to avoid distracting the reader. This omission in no way diminishes their contributions. Last but not least, names have also been omitted in a handful of cases where sources asked not to be quoted by name ahead of time as a condition of being interviewed, instances of which are noted in the text. No other names or facts have been changed.

Alexander Russo
Brooklyn, New York

PART ONE

..

DESPERATE MEASURES

1

DESPERATE SCHOOL REFORM SUPERSTAR

In spring 2007, school reform superstar Steve Barr was, unknown to most, deeply frustrated and thinking about taking a break. At the time, pretty much everyone thought of Barr as a phenomenal success, a charismatic visionary, a force of nature when it came to improving education for poor children. But he'd gained some weight and wasn't eating well. He was working too hard, traveling too much, and missing his family. Sometimes he lost his temper more than he meant to. Maybe, after more than a half a dozen hard years getting his nonprofit organization, Green Dot, off the ground, Barr was just worn out. When Green Dot moved into generic downtown offices, he insisted on having a swinging glass door built connecting his office out to the gravel deck outside (and paid half the costs), just to make being there more bearable. Maybe he'd spend time at his wife's vacation home in Taos, New Mexico, and do some writing. He needed to figure out what his next move was going to be.

What burdened Barr most was the realization that the most tangible, lofty-sounding goal his nonprofit set out to accomplish—starting one hundred new small high schools—wasn't really big enough to make a dent on the massive Los Angeles school district he hoped to change. A hundred new schools weren't going to have any real effect, and the model wasn't financially sustainable either. To reach that "tipping point" where the district started making its own changes, Green Dot needed to help fix some of the district's existing neighborhood high schools—hulking three-thousand-student behemoths with horrific dropout rates. Big high schools were where the greatest need was—as well as the kids and the facilities (and the money). But for all of Green Dot's efforts and Barr's political skills, he just couldn't convince the district to give him a chance, and the repeated failures were frustrating Barr in the extreme.

Six-foot-three and well over 200 pounds, Barr didn't look or act like most school reform types. He wasn't a suited-up consultant type or a crunchy social justice guy with a goatee. He didn't speak educationese or even have an education background. Relaxed and personable, he usually wore large, comfortable clothes—rumpled linen or cotton that looked as if it'd just been picked up off the bedroom floor—and an ancient Dodgers baseball cap pulled low over his flinty blue eyes. The former Cupertino High School basketball star worked on the 1984 Los Angeles Olympics and did advance work on several political campaigns before he cofounded Rock the Vote, a national youth voter registration effort, in 1990. Next came Green Dot, the outgrowth of Barr's search for something meaningful to do with the second half of his life (and a 1997 charter school visit with then-president Clinton). Graduation rates at the worst high schools could be as low as 5 percent. Good schools could get that number up to 50, 80, even 90 percent. Schools might not be able to solve all of kids' problems, but the best ones could make a dramatic difference.

So Barr decided he would start a nonprofit and begin opening schools.

Barr threw himself into the effort with speed and abandon—and remarkable success. Green Dot Public Schools launched in 1999 with the goal of opening one hundred small, successful charter high schools in the toughest parts of Los Angeles. Barr put up $100,000 of his own money to get things started and didn't take a salary for the first several years. He wasn't beholden to any particular educational fad or approach; he stole good ideas from wherever he could find them, took money from funders, and resisted expanding too quickly or becoming anyone's show pony.

The main thing he knew was that the schools many kids were going to now weren't as good as they could be, like the one he'd gone to in the Northern California town of Cupertino in the 1970s, the last years of California's heyday as the best public school system in the nation. Barr had grown up in a series of small apartments with his mother, younger brother, and—during high school—stepfather. The family moved several times during Barr's childhood, and he spent a year in foster care when he was five. His mother was a transplanted New Yorker whose Jewish upbringing showed up in Barr's tendency to use words like "vigorish." She often couldn't afford to buy him the right sneakers or jeans, but he got a good enough education and thrived in sports. They settled in Northern California, and Barr worked the concession stands at Stanford football games to earn extra money as a teenager. After graduating from Cupertino High, Barr made it from the local community college to UC Santa Barbara, where he graduated with a degree in political science.

Like many popular reform ideas over the past twenty years, Barr's schools featured a new idea, a distinctive twist—a gimmick, some thought: the teachers at Green Dot charter schools, like those at almost all traditional public schools, were unionized. Invented more than twenty years ago, charter schools are public schools free of charge and open to everyone. They have to follow most of the same safety rules, and their students have to take the same annual tests, but they're generally independent from the local school district when it comes to things like curriculum decisions and staffing. And most of them—roughly forty-four hundred in 2007–2008—are nonunion workplaces. Barr wanted his schools to be charters so that they wouldn't have to deal with the district bureaucracy, but he wanted them to be unionized because he thought that was the right thing to do and because he'd been involved in politics long enough to know how important labor was to any powerful movement. Unionization softened the resistance to charters.

Like many start-ups, Green Dot was for many years a fast-moving, informal operation. For a long time, Barr ran it out of his house in Venice, where a handful of staffers would come over to put out fires or work on writing charter applications or find space to house a new school. The teachers Green Dot hired were inexperienced, as were the principals. For the first several years, Green Dot didn't even have anyone with a strong education background on the staff. ("You know what they say," Barr said. "Better to have a hole than an asshole.") They found some classroom space, hired the best principal they could find, and handed him or her the keys. One school turned into five. Five schools turned into seven. Each new school started out with just one grade level—ninth—and then added a grade each year until it covered grades 9 through 12. Still, they served some of Los Angeles' poorest communities, and were lauded for graduation rates that were much better than the surrounding district schools. Along the way, Barr influenced the outcome of the citywide school board elections and made education a definitive issue in the 2005 Los Angeles mayor's race (won by Antonio Villaraigosa). In 2006, the *Los Angeles Times Magazine* named Barr one of the one hundred most powerful people in Southern California. A Southern California public radio commentator suggested—not entirely in jest—that Barr could get thousands of people to show up at a rally with a simple snap of his fingers. Things were going pretty well for him in his personal life, too. The inveterate bachelor finally got married and started a family. (Twenty years his junior, his wife-to-be met him at Burning Man and married him a few weeks after.) He moved out of the still-gritty beachside neighborhood of Venice and, eventually, into a spacious home in Silver Lake, a hip, hilly neighborhood located next to a reservoir near downtown Los Angeles.

••

Incapable of resting on his laurels, Barr pushed on toward bigger and more audacious schemes.

The idea of Green Dot helping run an existing public high school was brilliant, harebrained, desperate—akin to a small family chain of grocery stores saying it wanted to operate the local Walmart or Costco. Green Dot had been around less than a decade. Its rocketlike expansion had already stretched the organization to the limit. Turning around an existing school was the hardest thing to do in education—equivalent to stopping smoking two packs a day, losing a hundred pounds, *and* saving a long-broken relationship all at the same time. In failed schools there was so much history, so many bad habits, and so many ways to slip up. No surprise, then, that in education and in the private sector, half or more of turnarounds that are attempted failed to take hold or—even worse—were superficial makeovers. Much bigger and more established education organizations had tried—and often failed—at managing dysfunctional public schools in the past. One well-known charter organization, KIPP (Knowledge Is Power Program), tried doing a turnaround and vowed never to do them again.

Despite all these considerations, Barr was convinced that this was exactly what Green Dot needed to do. Barr's idea was to revamp all forty-six of LA's broken high schools in the Green Dot model—a strategy that could reach 75 percent of the high school students in the district within ten years. "This has to be for everyone," said Barr. "It's gotta be wall to wall." When racial violence kicked up at the overcrowded Jefferson High School in 2005, Barr seemed to have found an opening. He drove around the neighborhood surrounding the school, talking to parents and community leaders about rescuing Jefferson from its low test scores and high dropout rates. There were a lot of desperate, hard-working people out there who weren't being treated right by their schools, who'd been made promise after promise, only to be disappointed and forgotten. "You fall in love with these people," said Barr. He went to so many churches and neighborhood meetings and told the same stories so many times that he couldn't keep track. Sometimes his infant daughter came along, sleeping in the backseat of his car as he drove from place to place.

Barr was a disciplined campaigner, nearly always telling vivid stories, engaging emotionally with a range of audiences, rarely lapsing into abstract jargon. He gave witness to the dysfunction he saw and to a vision of how things could be better, and when he got worked up you could see the power of his vision come through: the urgency, the hope, the desire to show everyone wrong and the confidence that it could be done—that he could do it.

Using all his political skills and know-how, Barr organized a petition drive that garnered ten thousand signatures and, in

November 2005, pulled off a thousand-person "March of the Parents" delivering the signatures—and a slew of new charter school applications—to show the district they meant business. Green Dot would help the district fix Jefferson, or it would serve the community on its own by starting a bunch of new charter schools in the area, effectively siphoning kids away from Jefferson. For a few hours, Barr thought they'd done it. At a charter schools conference in Sacramento, staying at the Sheraton, he met a top district official in the morning to hammer out the details over coffee: Green Dot would share Jefferson with the district and the union, working to create small new schools on the campus. The two men shook hands, and Barr spent the rest of the day in a happy haze. Around five o'clock that afternoon, however, Barr got a call from the superintendent himself, a longtime Democratic lawmaker named Roy Romer, saying that he couldn't do the deal. Horrified and enraged at what he assumed was Romer's reluctance to cross the powerful teachers union, Barr found himself yelling at Romer over the phone. All the disappointment and desperation came flowing out of him. "We could have made history," he said.

••

The loss of Jefferson marked a turning point for Barr. He believed in what he was doing and in his own abilities to pull it off. He desperately wanted to improve the lives of the many children in Los Angeles who were attending subpar schools. But after the rejection at Jefferson, his efforts would become more aggressive and sometimes tinged with anger.

In September 2006, Green Dot opened five new schools around Jefferson. Half of the Jefferson parents entered the lottery to gain admission. But Barr was still shut out of the big game—the vast system of district schools—and was burning a lot of bridges along the way. The only other way to get a school was to take one by making use of an unusual provision in California law that allowed a school's teachers to "convert" a district school into an independent charter school by vote. A majority of tenured teachers at a school had to sign a petition requesting that the school be made independent from the district, and the district board had to approve the petition. The conversion process—a teacher trigger, essentially—had been used in a handful of relatively affluent parts of the city where parents and educators wanted independence from the district but didn't really feel they needed any outside help. The process hadn't ever been used to hand a desperately broken high school over to an outside charter organization. (The federal law called No Child Left Behind also allowed districts to convert failing schools into charters—without teacher input—though few districts had embarked on this route.)

If such a thing ever happened, it would have to be done over the strenuous objections of A. J. Duffy, head of the United Teachers of Los Angeles, which represented all the district teachers in the city and opposed charters—and Barr—with tremendous energy. (Duffy wasn't the only one who disliked Barr. An April 2007 column in the *Los Angeles Times* acknowledged that many thought of him as a "megalomaniacal publicity hound.") From Duffy's perspective, charters—even unionized ones like Green Dot—represented a threat to hard-won salary, benefits, and job protections. Green Dot teachers were organized through a competing union rather than with Duffy, for whom Barr had expressed a certain amount of hostility. In a December 2006 article chronicling the tensions between Green Dot and the teachers union, Barr was quoted complaining about Duffy's unsubstantiated criticisms. "It's like me saying, 'Duffy's a pig fucker.' Have I seen him fuck a pig? Do I have photos? No. So I can't say it."

Barr wasn't afraid of a fight. He knew that school reform was political, that elected officials responded to pressure and money (and media) more than ideas and appeals to altruism, and that the most intense conflicts in education weren't between Democrats and Republicans but rather among unions, charter school advocates, accountability hawks, and traditional educators. They were all trying to improve schools, but they didn't necessarily agree with each other. These were the competing "tribes" of American education Barr talked about bringing together. Such were the many contradictions of Steve Barr, the pugnacious unifier, the combative cooperator. He knew that trying to fix a broken neighborhood high school would be extremely difficult, and that the warring tribes might well turn against him. He knew he was worn out from all he'd already done. But he still wanted to give it a try—he still had to push forward. In spring 2007, the only question was whether anyone would give him a chance to take over a full-size Los Angeles high school and show the world what Green Dot could really do.

2

GETTING LOCKE

On Thursday, May 3, 2007, during a fairly routine school tour, Barr finally got his big break. Bush education secretary Margaret Spellings was doing a West Coast tour and made it a point to visit at least one charter school everywhere she went. For her visit to Los Angeles, she decided to go see a Green Dot school. She liked Barr's willingness to take on any and everyone to make schools better. "There are a lot of people talking about school reform, but they're many of them dinking around the edges," said Spellings. "But this is a china-breaking kind of enterprise." With Barr as her guide and a handful of reporters in tow, Spellings toured the campus and then sat down to talk to parents about the challenges of finding good schools for their children in South Central Los Angeles.

Frank Wells, the young principal of nearby Locke High School, stood in the back of the hot, overcrowded room listening to the emotional tales. The soft-spoken principal had a closely groomed goatee and a bright, earnest look in his eye. It was his first visit to a Green Dot school and his third year at Locke. Locke ranked high in student behavior and discipline problems, and was one of the poorest-performing schools in the city. The cruel joke in the neighborhood was that Locke students were so dumb that they couldn't even spell the name of their own school.

Toward the end of the meeting, Wells surprised everyone when he stepped forward and started speaking about his own frustrations at Locke. "I went to Locke thinking I could turn it around," said Wells, who spoke quietly and carefully. He had gotten the school off the top of the crime statistics list and was making slow but steady academic progress, but the district kept sending him ineffective tenured teachers who were extremely difficult to remove. "Nothing is going to change in the lives of [Locke's] kids unless we do something revolutionary overnight."

Wells had been saying much the same thing in private all year, but this time he was saying it out loud in front of a roomful of witnesses, including several reporters who were there covering Spellings's visit. It sounded as though Wells was calling out his employers in public, proposing a Green Dot takeover of the school—and committing professional suicide.

"There was an urgency to his voice," said *USA Today* education reporter Greg Toppo, there covering the Spellings visit. "He sounded like someone who was at the end of his rope."

The connections between Green Dot and Locke went back a few years. There were a few teachers at Locke who had wanted to make big changes at the school or if necessary start their own schools. One of them heard Barr give a speech in 2004 and came back to school talking about it. He and a colleague discussed the Green Dot model and then eventually called and invited Barr to come speak at Locke. A year later, Barr agreed to come to the school, and the teachers snuck him into an empty room after school, only to have the meeting broken up by a school administrator less than ten minutes in. A few days later, one of the teachers—Bruce Smith—heard Barr's spiel at another high school and returned to Locke a full-blown Green Dot enthusiast.

Two years later, the conversations about what to do to improve Locke had begun to bubble up again. Behind the scenes, Barr and the district had been trying to work out a cooperative arrangement for Green Dot to take over Locke, but the deal seemed to have stalled out as they always did. Dissatisfaction among teachers had grown stronger. Smith organized a meeting at the Watts Labor Community Action Center with Barr and as many of the best Locke teachers as he could persuade to attend. Nearly two dozen teachers showed up, going back and forth about Green Dot, the district, and the teachers union. The two main things that everyone agreed on were that the only time anyone from the district came out to do something for the school was when a kid got shot, and the only time anyone from the union came out was when Green Dot got mentioned. In the meantime, Smith was meeting with Wells in private, urging him to get in front of what seemed increasingly like an inevitable revolution. Wells was no fan at the start. He opposed the opening of Green Dot schools in the neighborhood around Locke, and criticized Green Dot at a faculty meeting. But his opinion was slowly changing. "At least, the students would not be subjected to bad teachers and a system that failed to provide a quality educational experience," said Wells. He and Barr met for dinner shortly afterwards at the Proud Bird restaurant next to Los Angeles International Airport and, as sometimes happens, found that they got along better than expected. (Or, at least, they found they had interests in common.) Both from Northern California, Wells and Barr were outsiders in South Central. At the end of the long meal, Barr invited Wells to come tour a Green Dot school and hear what parents had to say.

At first, Barr was upset about Wells's grandstanding at the Spellings event. "Right in the middle of the goddamn event he hijacks the meeting with this tirade," said Barr. Some of the

Green Dot supporters back at Locke were mystified by their principal's sudden-seeming change of heart. But Wells's remarks pushed them all into action. If Wells gave them access to the campus and supported their efforts, Green Dot might be able to persuade enough teachers to snatch the school away from the district and the union. The next morning, the headline in the *Los Angeles Times* was "Locke principal rips L.A. Unified." For Barr, all hopes of taking a breather were pushed to the side. If Green Dot won control of Locke, the organization would be embarking on its biggest challenge ever.

Over the weekend, Locke teachers started to prepare for the signature-gathering process. Green Dot sent a charter application. Smith, Wells, and another teacher made plans to circulate the petition sheets first thing on Monday morning. It turned out that only seventy-three of the teachers at the school were fully certified, tenured teachers assigned to the school with full voting rights; Green Dot supporters needed only thirty-seven signatures to gain control over the school. That morning, district officials were there in the breezeway, eyeing everyone suspiciously; undaunted, Green Dot supporters gathered twenty-six signatures the first day, spent the night worried that they would fall short of the mark or somehow find themselves barred from campus or suddenly transferred to a far-off school the next day, and pushed through the following morning. By lunchtime the next day, the pro–Green Dot group had gathered more than enough—sixty-five signatures in just two days, with forty-three signatures belonging to tenured faculty members. Smith and a colleague went to an off-campus Jack in the Box for lunch, and went home at the end of the day as usual. Wells stayed late to meet with his budget committee. It was nearly six o'clock when the meeting finished. Walking out of the meeting room, Wells saw that the area director was there—Wells's boss—who told him he was being reassigned to the district office and asked for Wells's keys—the educational equivalent of a cop being told to hand over his badge and gun or an office worker being asked to turn in her key card and ID badge. Wells refused to give up the keys without a receipt, and was then escorted out of the building. There was no opportunity for him to tell his teachers or explain to the kids. He never went back into the building. It was less than a week after he'd had publicly voiced support for Green Dot.

The district could remove Wells, but it was too late to stop the conversion process. After forty years, Locke would be taken away from the district that had long governed it, and turned into a charter school. Green Dot would lease the building from the district and operate the school independently—within the law. But, unlike most charter schools, Locke would remain the neighborhood attendance school for the area. That meant that anyone who wanted to attend had only to show up and prove they lived in the neighborhood. And Locke's teachers would remain unionized (albeit under a much different union agreement). The new Locke would be an "everyone's welcome" turnaround, a full-size unionized charter school.

Almost immediately afterwards, the events surrounding Locke's conversion were turned into myth. One story line was that Locke teachers had spontaneously risen up against the district. Another was that Barr had single-handedly engineered a revolt against the district. A third version was that Wells and his allies were responsible for the coup. In reality, Green Dot had been looking for a school to take over for more than a year and a half, ever since Jefferson. Teachers at Locke had been watching Green Dot for even longer, recruiting Barr as much as he was recruiting them. The mating dance would take over four years from start to finish, and was a pairing of mutual convenience and desperation more than love at first sight. But most of these complexities were neatly forgotten or underplayed in the following weeks and months. That summer, Green Dot got the first of what would be several major write-ups in the national press. The *New York Times* described Barr as an audacious maverick who'd been waging "a guerrilla war for control of this city's chronically failing high schools." Locke was described as a school in disarray, desperate for a savior.

Before Green Dot took over, the school had to make it through a series of setbacks. First, the district and union persuaded seventeen of the teachers who had signed the conversion petition to rescind, forcing Green Dot supporters inside the school to go through the signature-gathering exercise a second time. Then it took another four months (and a new set of elected board members) for the school board to approve the conversion. At that point—September 2007—it was too late for Green Dot to take over the school for the 2007–2008 school year. Locke would remain a district school for one last, long year. Green Dot would take over on July 1, 2008. During the intervening months, the delicate relationship between those teachers and community members who had made the handover possible and those who would now take over the school would become increasingly unbalanced.

3

YEAR IN LIMBO

Located just off of the 110 Freeway, Locke High School sat due east of Los Angeles International Airport. All day you could see jumbo airplanes passing high overhead in the blue sky over campus. The neighborhood was largely residential, left relatively unscathed by the 1992 Rodney King riots. Still, the area felt isolated, desolate, low-slung—a long way off from LA's vibrant downtown, the beaches and palm trees of the breezy West Side, or the compact buzz of East LA. Still technically in Los Angeles—but not, technically, in Watts proper—Locke stood only a few blocks away from the outer edge of the official city line. Locke was at the very edge of the school district, on the brink of falling off the map. Yet there was a certain beauty to the place—a realness, a sense of solidity. The single-story ranch-style homes were generally neat, with well-kept gardens. Stores with hand-drawn signs—Addy's Bakery, Dan's Mini Market, and the Centro Familiar Cristiano—lined Avalon Boulevard, to the east of campus. A painted taco stand on the corner was a student and teacher favorite, as were the tiny food carts that appeared at dismissal time.

Named after the first African American Rhodes scholar, Alain Leroy Locke High School was built after the Watts riots and for many years was a source of pride and a starting point for many of the community's leaders. The school featured what was then considered a state-of-the-art campus, complete with a library, theater space, athletic fields, and a multipurpose auditorium that could be used for performances or movies. Its sports teams and its marching band were the envy of many other schools, and along the way Locke graduated not one but two baseball hall-of-famers (Eddie Murray and Ozzie Smith). Other famous graduates included the model and actor Tyrese Gibson, professional women's basketball player Cynthia Cooper, and musicians Patrice Rushen and Gerald Albright. Everyone in the neighborhood went to Locke or worked there or knew someone who did. Even though Locke wasn't the best-known school in the area (that honor probably went to nearby Crenshaw), at least it wasn't the most fearsome, either. (That designation probably went to Jordan, located across from a set of fearsome housing projects.)

With its well-worn light-blue paint and dingy white trim, the main administrative building looked like a tropical hotel during the dry season. The blue-and-white marquee out front read "Locke High School, Home of the Successful Saints." (The school logo was a stick figure with a halo above its head, though more often than not Locke uniforms employed an ornate "L" and a fleur-de-lis as the school symbol.)

In theory, handing Locke over to Green Dot would almost immediately restore the school to its former glory. However, that was not to be. Neither the district nor Green Dot took full responsibility for the school during the months that followed. Unexplained budget cuts reduced campus security, changes to Locke's attendance boundaries upset the delicate balance of factions among students on campus, and principals at other high schools started sending Locke kids who'd been transferred under Wells back to their home school.

It didn't take long after the petition signing for things to start going wrong. Shortly after Wells was removed in May, racial tensions erupted during a lunchtime press conference Green Dot held outside. ("Barr had inadvertently started a riot at the school he promised to save," noted *Forbes* magazine.) The disorder returned with a vengeance during the start of the 2007–2008 year. Every square inch of the school would be tagged—door handles, metal railings, tables, windowsills, outside walls. The school would average nearly five suspensions a day. By one count, there were sixteen fights in the first two weeks of the new school year alone.

Perhaps the most troubling incident of the fall took place during a long, chaotic Friday in October, when an assistant principal named Alfonso (Alfee) Enciso had a run-in with a new kid he'd never seen before, a small Latino boy who didn't much like being told to go to class.

"I'll smoke you," the angry kid told Enciso. "You don't know who I am."

Some Locke longtimers thought that Enciso didn't know what he was doing. "That dude didn't have a clue," said Wayne Crawford, a dean and football coach at the school. "Not. A. Clue." But after nearly a decade working in Watts, the forty-nine-year-old Enciso wasn't all that worried about the threatening words. He had good relationships with many of the kids on campus, and overheated reactions like this weren't all that uncommon. Most of the time, they were empty threats. But Wells was gone, Enciso was relatively new to Locke, and—though he didn't know it yet—he wasn't going to be there much longer. Enciso handed the defiant kid off to a new dean to handle the matter, but then a fight broke out among another group of kids, and then another, and another. In the confusion, the boy who'd threatened Enciso slipped away. Toward the end of the school day, as Enciso was headed back toward the main administrative building, the boy he'd confronted earlier and a few other kids ran up behind Enciso, swinging wild punches at the administrator's head. Enciso ducked out of the way of the first swing just in time; a second punch grazed his head. Then it was over. Other administrators pulled off the attackers.

The incident didn't seem like much to Enciso, but the interim principal brought in to replace Wells thought otherwise. He told Enciso to report to the district office on Monday rather than coming back to campus. Enciso had been accused of grabbing a boy the year before. During this year's uncertain situation, the principal felt that he had to err on the side of caution about bringing Enciso back. Administrators gave Enciso a farewell party at a nearby Mexican restaurant about a month after he left the school—one of few school administrators honored this way. After Enciso left, the rumor persisted that he'd gotten his jaw broken and that an ambulance had been called to take him to the hospital. The story wasn't true, according to Enciso, but it might as well have been for the amount of people who believed it so. And the fact remained that a group of kids had attacked an administrator on campus during the school day.

Enciso thought that former principal Frank Wells was orchestrating the disorder from off campus, trying to punish the district and get Green Dot to give him his job back. "He really believed that getting kids to fight would get him his job back," said Enciso. "He had this image of riding back to Locke on a white horse to save the school." Others, like English teacher Joshua Beardall, thought that Green Dot was indirectly at fault, watching from the sidelines as the school fell apart. "Maybe they wanted it to look as bad as it could," said Beardall.

••

Originally one of Green Dot's strongest allies, English teacher Bruce Smith sounded less and less confident about Green Dot as the limbo year went on. Blond with a high forehead, he had three kids, a mortgage, and an elderly parent he helped take care of. He crossed his legs at the thigh rather than at the ankle and wore starched pants and pressed shirts. He had an amazing recall for dates and facts. He'd taught at Locke for the last seven years and in Korea for seven years before that. He was a longtimer by current Locke standards, though he didn't come from the community. And, nearly as soon as Wells was removed from campus the previous spring, Smith was stripped of leadership assignments, such as his role as assessment coordinator, and was required instead to patrol the trailers and football bleachers in the back corner of the campus. He couldn't be fired (thanks to the contract negotiated by the union he and many others had come to loathe), but the contract didn't stop the school district from removing any perks and replacing them with undesirable assignments. The union wasn't especially protective of members it considered traitors. It was hot, dusty, and potentially dangerous work he was given, considering how unruly things could get at the school. At one point after one of the deans quit, Smith was assigned to monitor a room full of truant kids without one of the handheld two-way radios used to communicate on campus.

Along the way, Smith was getting glimpses inside Green Dot that he didn't much like. Over the summer, Green Dot had received a $7.8 million pledge from the Bill and Melinda Gates Foundation to help fix Locke. In September, when Green Dot threw a big party in celebration of its approval as the new management at Locke, Smith overheard two Green Dot staffers laughing about an extremely overweight teacher at Locke who had been recruited to sign the Green Dot petition. They needed any and every signature they could get. She had hopes of keeping her job and her convenient parking spot by a first-floor classroom. Now they were laughing "as if there was never any possibility that she could work for them," recalled Smith. "My jaw just fell on the floor. What have I done, working with these people who are laughing at us?"

Making matters worse, communication from Green Dot to the school was informal and inconsistent for much of the fall. How many schools would there be on campus? When would Green Dot decide who got to stay at the school? Was it true that there wouldn't be a football team anymore? No one knew the answers. It took more than two months for Green Dot to secure some space on campus—an abandoned shop classroom that they could use for planning meetings and interviews. But then, for another month, the space went unused.

Green Dot wasn't ignoring Locke intentionally. For reasons that would later become apparent, the organization just didn't have enough bandwidth to maintain its twelve existing schools, get ready for the year ahead, and keep in touch with the teachers and community members on campus at the same time. Along the way, a lot of toes were stepped on.

"We took the school over, and those teachers got shit on for a year," said Barr, who blamed the district for the chaos. "There was nothing. No one was responding. It just lapsed for a year."

So, instead of a year spent building excitement and momentum, it was a year of backsliding and confusion. Teachers like Smith just had to gut it out. They could see the school environment deteriorating and the momentum from the previous year slipping away (along with what few effective teachers Locke had remaining). But there was nothing they could do. "I know more than anyone else," said Smith, "and I don't know as much as I'd like."

Just as disheartening for the Locke community was hearing the school being torn down over and over again in the media and around the neighborhood. Students like Michael McElveen, then a junior, wrote that they were constantly asked questions including "Why had I chosen Locke high school? Which gang ran Locke? Was it true teachers hung in the halls and skipped class? Was everyone stupid at Locke?" There was precious little attention to teachers "who cared dearly about their performance, our performance and the performance of the school as a whole," or to students who "confronted academic and societal boundaries and succeeded." Failure and dysfunction were becoming the face of Locke even more than they had ever been—and in many ways even more than was deserved. Locke was never, despite all assertions to the contrary, really such a hotbed of gang activity compared to other nearby schools. Its scores were low; its teaching staff was a mess. But things weren't as bad as they were being made to seem. (Or at least they hadn't been until now.)

Behind the scenes, there was a nagging worry that the Green Dot effort would end up just like all the others before it. "Reforms and programs have come and gone as quickly as the teachers and administrators assigned to implement them," wrote Donna Foote, whose 2008 book *Relentless Pursuit* followed the lives of four young teachers at the school. What was Green Dot going to do that hadn't already been tried? Why would Green Dot keep its promises when nobody else had? Over the years, it seemed as though everything had already been done: changing principals, creating small schools within the building, bringing in different class materials, improving professional development. But none of it seemed to make a big dent. As at many schools, Locke had a whole system of things that were going wrong, and a troubling ability to derail improvement efforts. Fixing the problems at

Locke wasn't going to be as easy as pointing them out. In most cases, things were wrong for a reason. You had to fix the reason, too. In the meantime, two out of ten kids didn't show up to school every day. Kids who showed up didn't go to class, or went to classes and found that not all of their teachers were still trying.

4

UNLIKELY LEADER

Only in December did Green Dot finally start holding advisory meetings on campus and using the planning room regularly. There were a handful of principals in training who were being readied to run the small schools on campus, but Green Dot still didn't have anyone to lead the school that would house all the sophomores, juniors, and seniors who already attended Locke. This would be the biggest of the seven schools that would make up the "new" Locke High School—and probably the most difficult to manage. Toward the end of that month, administrators went to Veronica ("Ronnie") Coleman, one of Green Dot's principal trainees, and asked her if she wanted the job.

"Oh, hell no," was Coleman's response. "No, no, no, no, no."

The forty-something Coleman was a veteran assistant principal from Long Beach, a widely renowned school district just to the south of Los Angeles, and had signed up for the Green Dot training program as a way to—finally—get her own school. She had straight, sandy hair and a long, slender face; skin that flushed pink when she was impatient or angry; and a loping, almost bow-legged walk—the product of a childhood on a Michigan farm and years playing sports. But she had signed up to run a "traditional"

Green Dot school—the small-school model that meant starting one grade at a time, growing year by year. The job she was being offered now was a whole 'nother thing.

Originally named the Locke Launch to College Academy, the cumbersome name of the school Coleman was being asked to head was quickly shortened to its initials, LLCA, then LCA, then finally, on account of its size, just "Big Locke." Running Big Locke was, without a doubt, going to be the hardest and least desirable job in the entire Locke turnaround effort—not only because of its initial challenges of size but also because there would be little reward. Under the Green Dot transformation plan, Big Locke would eventually cease to exist. Instead of taking in new kids each year, like a normal school, it would phase itself out over three years, as each group of kids graduated. The small new schools on campus—the "baby" Lockes, they would be called—would take all the incoming Locke ninth graders each year, growing as Big Locke was shrinking. It would have been enormously simpler to set up five schools on campus that each would have served the entire span of grades right from the start and weren't constantly growing or shrinking, but Green Dot had decided that this complicated, Rube Goldberg kind of setup was the school's best chance to break free of the dysfunctional student culture at Locke and to build excellence and accountability from teachers. As a result, Big Locke would cease to exist after three years. There was no future in the job, no glory, no nothing.

Even if she'd wanted the job, Coleman was an extremely unlikely choice. There was nothing flashy about her, nothing that signaled that she might be a strong school leader. She didn't talk a big game or try to make herself stand out. She didn't make big speeches. She was quick to take blame and slow to take credit. She had never run a school before. She was a middle-aged rookie principal from the Midwest who didn't want the job.

As winter break approached, however, Coleman couldn't stop thinking about the opportunity. She drove down to the school before and after work and wandered the streets. She parked in front of the school and just sat there in her car observing the activity going on near the front gate. She watched as kids strolled into school long after classes started. She saw cops rousting teens who were drinking across from the school at 10 A.M. Even during the middle of the day, there were so many kids coming and going that the entrance to the school looked like a busy subway station. It was clear to Coleman that Locke was a mess; she didn't have to go inside to see that. But at the same time she realized what an exciting challenge it would be to run Big Locke, to clean up the mess. It didn't hurt that the mild-mannered Coleman was a bit of an adrenaline junkie. "No one had ever really done this before at this kind of scale," she said. "And I'm not very good at shrinking from challenges." A few days later, she accepted the job. She'd actually set foot on campus only once.

Starting in January, shortly after the holiday break, Coleman began going onto campus and wandering around the school. Things being the way they were, no one asked her who she was, or really cared where she went. There were unfamiliar faces on campus all the time—replacement teachers, district officials, school supply salesmen. Locke teachers and students might wonder who she was, but didn't bother to find out. Being unknown meant Coleman could get a realistic take on how the school worked. She just walked the halls, peeking in on classrooms and listening to what kids and teachers were saying through the doors. Sometimes she saw kids braiding hair or gambling. Other times she overheard them talking about *Macbeth*. It was that way for the first month or two. She would show up, wander around. She couldn't stop coming back, even though she wasn't yet formally assigned to the school.

"I got kind of obsessed with coming here," said Coleman. "I came and hung out a lot." It was endlessly fascinating, alternately horrifying and inspiring.

Later that month, Green Dot finally scheduled a job fair for Locke faculty who wanted to meet with the new principals Green Dot had hired. Coleman's appointment was still under wraps, and people at Locke were asking, "Where was Frank Wells?" But no one was entirely sure. For the past six months, Wells had been working with Green Dot at the home office, thinking that something good was going to happen at Locke and that he'd be a part of it. Of late, however, Wells had been hearing rumors from Locke that Green Dot was going to use its own principals or hire from outside. Wells wanted to find out from Barr face-to-face whether any of it was true.

In February, Wells and Barr met for lunch at the hotel across from Green Dot's downtown offices. Wells asked Barr straight out if it was true that he was out of the running for a leadership position at Locke, and Barr told him that indeed it was the case. "I suspected some things that were going on, but I still thought that Steve wouldn't do this," said Wells. "But all the rumors turned out to be true. It was a whole different Steve Barr and a whole different Green Dot organization."

According to Wells, Barr's reason was that if Wells returned as principal, it would compete with the focus on Green Dot. "Frank Wells brings too much attention," said Wells.

What had happened? Once a highly publicized part of the conversion effort, Wells fell victim to second thoughts from Green Dot, based in large part on the discovery that teachers' opinions about him were deeply divided. "Either you loved him or you couldn't stand his ass," said one teacher who asked not to be identified. It wasn't a simple decision for Green Dot to make. Some within the organization felt that they had to give Wells a leadership position, that it would look bad and break commitments if he wasn't part of the new Locke. There was a short but intense debate at the home office over what to do. But everyone who wanted to come back had to reapply for his or her job—there were no exceptions—and in the end Wells wasn't picked. After the school year ended, Green Dot would sever its relationship with him entirely.

The news that Wells wasn't going to be part of the turnaround hit music teacher Reggie Andrews hard. The tall, handsome educator was raised in the neighborhood and had taught at Locke since its second year of existence, with only a couple of short breaks. (Along the way, he'd cowritten and produced the Dazz Band's early 1980s hit, "Let It Whip.") "No one is more connected to the Locke community than me," said Andrews. The thirty-nine-year veteran felt that he had been instrumental in supporting the changeover from the district to Green Dot and had assumed that Wells would be back on campus the following fall. Now, that apparently wasn't going to happen; Wells was being left by the side of the road.

"Dr. Wells had gotten a lot of signatures for Green Dot, but he had no voice in terms of how this implementation of the new Locke was going to take shape," said Andrews. "Over 50 percent of the teachers who signed thought that Wells was on board."

What troubled Andrews wasn't just that Wells was out of the running but also who his replacement was going to be: that white woman who'd been wandering around for the past couple of months. Increasingly, teachers and staff at Locke started calling out to Coleman, "Hey, Green Dot. I want to talk to you about something." Everyone had suggestions and questions, and many were angling for information about the future. Andrews wasn't one of them. He thought Coleman was a bad choice, and was dismayed that there had been no community input into her selection. Over and over in the past, Green Dot had promised that there would be community input, but then all of a sudden the Locke community was being informed that principals would be assigned—just as the district used to do, just as so many other outsiders had done over the years. "So many people come to the Watts community," said Andrews. "Everybody says what they need to say to get what they want to get."

Andrews wasn't the only member of the Locke community to be suspicious of Green Dot. There was a small group who were unable to make the leap—understandably prone to taking offense and finding fault (and given ample opportunity to do so during Green Dot's slipshod handling of the transition year). At times it seemed as though they almost wanted Green Dot to fail, just to prove the point that Locke couldn't rely on anyone. Not everyone was as reluctant to trust outsiders as Andrews. The majority seemed remarkably quick to take new people in, accepting and hoping despite all the knowledge of past disappointments, responding to the attention and effort from Green Dot with enthusiasm and trust. They had no other choice, really. They couldn't afford to be cynical or skeptical.

In late March, Coleman walked into Andrews's cluttered office in the heart of campus and finally sat down with him. She hadn't met Andrews before—there were no formal announcements and introductions being organized by Green Dot—but she set up the meeting when she heard he was unhappy. She wanted to hear his concerns from him directly and, if possible, to reassure him that she could, with his help, do the job.

But that wasn't going to happen. "It's nothing personal," said Andrews. "But you weren't chosen by the staff here, you don't have any experience as a principal, and you don't come from our community. I don't believe you're the best fit for the job, and I will fight you coming here."

Andrews' voice wasn't raised. There wasn't any heat in his face. A passerby would have thought they could have been talking

about the weather. But the frank words were cutting, and felt
to Coleman as being about race and gender as much as experience and self-determination. She was used to people intimating
that maybe she—"a little white girl from the Midwest," as she
described herself—couldn't handle the jobs she'd been given, but
had never experienced anything this overt (and never expected
it would be delivered in terms that were so eerily calm). She
could feel her face flushing; she tried to keep calm. She said she
appreciated his candor and understood his concerns, and hoped
she would get the chance to work with him and prove his worries
unfounded. Then she walked out of the room.

In truth, Wells wasn't Andrews's only concern, or even his
main issue. (Andrews's first choice for running Locke was the
Locke alumna who'd been principal for three years before the
district replaced her with Wells.) He worried in particular that
Green Dot wouldn't provide a strong program for Locke's male
students—specifically its African American boys, who were, as
at many schools, failing and being expelled disproportionately.
Andrews was focused on making sure that boys weren't left out
of the plans for Locke. He pitched a boys-only school, a music
program, a vocational program, a sports program. He encouraged
Green Dot to consider a peer's online learning program for kids
who needed to make up lots of credits. Some of the adults at the
school had piloted a program called Men of Locke, whose motto
was "boys will be boys, but men must be men." Andrews hoped
that something along those lines—expanded even—would be
part of the new Locke, something to help pull up the young men
who were, he felt, pulling everyone back.

"What do you have in place for black males besides football?"
Andrews asked Barr in one of their last telephone conversations.

"How about teaching them how to read?" responded Barr,
whose patience for Andrews had diminished since the exciting

weeks when they'd been working together to wrest control of Locke from the district. ,

A related concern was that Green Dot wouldn't serve the same spectrum of kids as Locke had in the past. If Green Dot succeeded, it was said, it would do so largely by sifting out the most difficult kids—the knuckleheads, the troublemakers, the kids with serious special education needs. There was no strong tradition of charter schools serving any and all kids who showed up, and little confidence that Green Dot could pull it off.

"It won't be the same kids," said the doubters.

As it turned out, Green Dot wouldn't do any of the things Andrews and others suggested besides the online learning program. And Andrews wouldn't get to stay at Locke, either. He didn't want to leave; he tried to stay. He was proud to have helped wrest the school away from a district and a union that seemed not to care about the kids of Watts. But he would end up turning down the job he was offered because it didn't include music (and was, according to Green Dot, subsequently withdrawn). "Reggie wouldn't go along with the things they were saying, so they didn't keep him on," said a Locke veteran. When Andrews finally realized at the last possible moment in August that he wasn't coming back to Locke, it was heartbreaking but, as he saw it, necessary. He packed up the large office full of all the papers and memorabilia you'd expect from more than three decades of teaching—awards, certificates, trophies, photographs—got assigned to another district high school, and, over the next two years, would watch the Locke turnaround from afar, forced to wear a visitor's badge when he came on campus, helpless to save some of the kids he'd worked with so closely.

"If I was staying at Locke, that would have meant I was agreeing with Green Dot," he said. "I left because I did not agree. I left symbolically."

5

SCRAMBLING FOR TEACHERS

Coleman was getting a late start, had to deal with grumbling surrounding her selection as head of Big Locke, and faced an enormous job. Although she had no formal access to the teachers on campus during the day (the school still officially belonged to the district), she was supposed to set up all the systems of a full-size school, from scratch, working out of a makeshift office on the back side of campus, while the regular school was winding down the year. She had to hire seventy teachers for a school that she did not yet have control over, which meant interviewing hundreds. For much of the year, she didn't have any staff and couldn't make formal job offers. Job candidates who came to interview entered through the front gate and were directed to the back office where Green Dot was based. The space they'd given her was bare of anything besides a few desks and chairs. She had to go off campus just to send a fax.

It wasn't just Coleman who was under the gun. Less than a decade into its existence, Green Dot had to find principals for seven new schools, a plant manager, and a security company, and to figure out food services and facilities cleaning too. When and how would the district give Green Dot access to student files? No one knew. Perhaps the biggest weight was on Green Dot's operations team, led by former Bain & Company consultant Marco Petruzzi. Doing a big turnaround had been his idea, in part, and now he had one on his hands. It was already clear that Green Dot was struggling when it came to messaging and outreach. Could it perform any better when it came to hiring, organizing, and setting up a school, much less providing quality instruction to kids in classrooms?

One of Coleman's most immediate challenges was to figure out what to do with the longtime clerical staff she was obliged to hire under the deal between the district and Green Dot. This was one of the concessions Green Dot had made in order to get through the contentious conversion process the year before. They were, in the parlance of education, "must hires." They had to go somewhere. (The special education teachers were also all staying on, but only for the first year.) But many of these clerks, campus aides, and secretaries didn't seem to have the computer skills or work habits that Green Dot thought were going to be needed.

Coleman first encountered Virendia Burnett walking around the school with a fistful of keys, a radio, and a hapless junior clerk in tow with a handcart stacked tall with reams of copy paper. Burnett was a slender, stylish dresser who tended toward matched outfits and high heels. "She had fifty keys and was barking into her radio," said Coleman. "I asked her what she did at Locke, and she told me she did a little bit of everything." But Burnett wasn't really doing anything, as far as Coleman could tell. And she seemed obsessed with the public address system. ("Anyone driving a light-blue Toyota needs to move. You're blocking me in, and I need to go to lunch.") Burnett was also making a lot of money—money that Green Dot couldn't afford to pay her. So Coleman did what any savvy administrator would do: she tried to talk Burnett out of coming back, telling her that the work was going to be hard and that she'd have to take a salary cut. Maybe she should think about finding another spot with the district.

Deciding whether to stay wasn't an easy decision for Burnett. It made her angry the way some adults at the school had gotten used to thinking of the students as little more than cash in their pockets. "If the kids stay dumb and stupid, then there's more money for them," she said. But Barr had won her over earlier in the year, when he helped the drill team with sparkling gold and blue uniforms. "I'm staying here," she said. "That man kept his word."

What did Burnett say, according to Coleman? "That's OK. This is my school. I'll adjust." Others still weren't sure about what they were going to do. Even though Locke had been struggling for so long, people came up to Burnett and asked her why she was "working for *them*?" It wasn't clear what Burnett could or would do in the new Locke; Coleman decided to give her a job in her own office out of consideration to the rest of her team.

Coleman's other big challenge was figuring out what to do about current Locke teachers. The previous year, more than half of the tenured faculty had signed onto the petition, not knowing with any certainty if they'd be rehired or whether their health benefits would be available or what would happen to them if the petition failed and they were left exposed to a district and union that could be unsympathetic and punitive in the extreme. The petition had stated that "the existing staff of Locke High School will fill much of the open positions on campus," but there were no guarantees. It had been, as the *Economist* called it, an "astonishing gesture"—not just one or two individuals risking their own futures but more than three dozen tenured teachers. It was a group sacrifice made not at the spur of the moment but after hours if not days of consideration. They'd put their careers at risk for an unproven nonprofit. But that didn't necessarily make them good candidates to work at the new Locke. Among these were a handful of dedicated, effective teachers who were working just as hard this year as they had been in the past. But Locke also had a slew of misfit and incompetent teachers who'd plagued Wells. All in all, Locke had "Thirty of the worst teachers in the district," said one administrator, "lazy, incompetent, defiant, 'didn't give a shit' teachers." There were teachers who were absent 80 days out of a 180-day year, and nearly a score of them with "red dot" warnings on their personnel files. For some, the game was to get as many special assignments as possible and teach as little as you could. Each job title—lead teacher, union rep, coordinator, committee member—meant extra salary and reduced teaching. These were the burned-out teachers Wells had been unable to remove, whose presence had prompted him to turn against the district and help Green Dot.

As winter turned to spring, it became clear that many Locke veterans who had voted in favor of the conversion wouldn't return. Some didn't want to stay. Others wanted to stay but couldn't afford to give up their health benefits and pensions. A few wanted to stay but didn't get hired. In the end, just eighteen of thirty-eight permanent staff members who voted for Green Dot would end up returning the following year. In their place, Coleman hired young, untenured teachers, many of whom would be new to the school and to teaching. For those who'd wanted to stay, it wasn't the outcome they expected or thought they deserved.

"I guess I sacrificed my job for these kids," says Frank Wiley, a teacher and dean who voted for Green Dot but wasn't offered a position at the new school.

In future months, Barr would say that the teachers had voted in favor of Green Dot knowing that they were unlikely to be rehired, sacrificing their own situations (if not their jobs) for the sake of the kids. "They were good people who didn't want to come back," he said. "It was such a heroic act—they were just so fed up it didn't matter anymore." Unfair or merely undiplomatic, the outcome was a loud warning to teachers at other schools who were considering following Locke's lead and petitioning for independence from the district. Why take the risk if you weren't going to be able to stay at the school you voted to liberate?

As reality began to set in, it became hard for people to come to work and put in a good effort knowing that they were unlikely to be around in a few weeks or months. There was a lot of confusion and anger among the staff, and the mood on campus got worse and worse as the end of the year approached. A handful of stalwarts were attempting to hold it all together until Green Dot took over, wanting to give the kids as good a year as possible. But many teachers had lost whatever morale they may have had once the end approached. They'd thrown in the towel and weren't even trying any more. It was as though a switch had been turned off, and in an instant teachers and staff went from caring to not caring. Many filled their last weeks with movies. Some days it seemed as though there were more movies shown at Locke than at the nearby Magic Johnson Cineplex. Others let kids hide out in their classrooms all day for a quarter. There was a mass tossing up of hands. "Let Green Dot sort it out," teachers said.

As morale plummeted among teachers and staff, a sense of menace that had been apparent since the beginning of the year grew more palpable in the halls. The cafeteria was a mess, with students leaving the place looking like a dump site. Kids weren't going to class, but weren't leaving campus either. There were a lot of chases and kids hopping fences back and forth off and onto the grounds. At one point administrators put black paint on the tops of fences as a way of revealing kids who'd been ditching. No one smiled. Teachers grew cautious about addressing students they didn't already know from class. The feeling was that someone was going to get hurt. There was an ominous surge of "slashing"—rival groups crossing out each other's graffiti. They burned the snack stand. They burned the theater space. They burned the viewing stand above the bleachers. This was the old Locke, only worse. It wasn't all Green Dot's fault. The district had cut security and seemed to be doing as little as possible to help Locke get through this last year. A few weeks later, the superintendent of the school district would admit, "We neglected this school." Indeed, what was taking place at Locke wasn't just mindless vandalism; it was students telling the adults that that they'd been abandoned, that they weren't being taken care of. They were sending a signal.

Finally—not a moment too soon—school ended on June 19, followed by a graduation ceremony that was, par for the course, a bit of a mess. Fewer than four hundred kids would graduate out of a class that had started out with more than fifteen hundred. The ceremony had to be halted a couple of times when family members started coming out onto the field before the speeches and awards were completed Of these graduates, fewer than a hundred had passed enough courses to be eligible to apply to a four-year state school like Cal State Northridge.

On their own, teachers and administrators held a year-end party at which Locke veterans gathered together one last time. One of them, a thirty-five-year counselor, among many who were being forced to leave, cried as she danced to the 1970s disco music. "What are you going to do with these people?" asked English teacher Smith, who was also leaving. "Nearly everyone at Green Dot is bright, young, and successful. They have almost no experience of failure or disappointment."

"This could be the next Lewis and Clark," said the interim principal, a district veteran who would go back into retirement at the end of the year. "Or it could end up as road kill."

This was the end of the old Locke. It was also, though few saw it at the time, the end of the old Green Dot. But first, there was the riot.

6

THE GATE

Before the riot, there was a dance. Each day for the last few weeks of school, administrators allowed kids to go into Hobbs Hall, the auditorium next to the covered eating area, and enjoy some music for the price of just a dollar. The lunchtime dances were a way to occupy the kids during the long lunch period—few of them ate the awful "county" food provided for them anyway—and to speed the long weeks between spring break and graduation. And for a few days it worked: music boomed from the PA system, kids goofed around, danced with their girlfriends and boyfriends, or stood at the edges watching each other.

It was Friday, May 9, 2008, just a few days past Cinco de Mayo, a day of celebration of Mexican culture (also informally known as a day for black and Latino students in the neighborhood to settle grudges). All year long, things had been unsettled on campus. The day began with a midmorning fight between two boys, both African American. Fighting wasn't anything new at Locke (or, unfortunately, at many big high schools). Counselors warned administrators that trouble might be brewing, but the warnings weren't passed along. Those standing in the quad at lunchtime had only a vague sense of tension.

"It was one of those days, you kind of felt it," said Officer Dwayne Palacio, one of two uniformed Los Angeles Unified School District police officers assigned to the school, who stood out in plain sight at the edge of the quad during lunch, making their presence known.

The quad was a large, enclosed space in the middle of campus, with covered walkways going around its perimeter and a big swath of grass—and a bunch of thorny rosebushes—in the middle. Alongside the two officers were a handful of campus aides and administrators. Lunch was the riskiest time of the day on campus, with the school's entire student population—theoretically as many as twenty-five hundred kids—gathered in the same place. Fridays could be especially lively.

Sometimes, fights were preplanned events. Students would videotape the brawls. Then they'd upload the movies to YouTube or MySpace. There were usually an agreed-on number of guys (usually five or ten) matched against an equal number. Most spontaneous campus fights were highly contained "one-on-ones." Students might gather around and hoot encouragement or instructions when students "got down," but they generally didn't join in. Eventually the combatants would tire or run or get hauled away by a campus aide or administrator. If caught, the combatants were cited, suspended, and sent home.

But during this particular lunchtime, nothing happened. Kids—most of them black—congregated either in the auditorium or out near the big tree favored by the football team. Others—many of them Latino—were scattered around the quad and close to the handball courts. The only things out of place that day were the groups of black and Hispanic boys walking around the lunch area and the quad. They were doing nothing but circling and eyeing each other.

The lunch period ended without any confrontation, and for a moment everyone thought danger had passed. Roughly half the kids headed toward the big three-story building that housed most of the school's classrooms. Others headed down Saint Street, the utility road going through campus, toward the clusters of bungalows that served as classrooms on the other side of campus. Then all of a sudden, no more than twenty feet in front of the two police officers, a group of African American kids started talking trash with a group of Hispanic kids. (Or maybe the Latino kids started it—accounts vary.) They weren't trying to conceal what they were doing, and no one was backing down.

"Those guys are about to fight," said Officer Brian Terry, Palacio's partner.

"This is going to be a big one," said one of the longtime campus aides.

A gregarious sophomore named Anthony was turning to walk down Saint Street and go to class when he heard someone behind him, cussing him out unprovoked, using the n-word. The boy was backed by a group.

"I heard somebody say, 'Fuck all black people,'" said Anthony, a member of the football team. "I turned around and saw that it was this little guy. I mean he was *little*. I know he's not talking to *me*. But he was, and he and his guys wanted to fight."

Anthony kicked off his slippers—black plastic flip-flops favored by some of the football players—and put his back up against the fence so that no one could get behind him.

Chain-link fences were everywhere on the campus, separating different parts of the school and—theoretically—keeping kids from getting into places they weren't supposed to go. Most of the fences were fixed in place—surrounding the handball courts, for example. But each area had a gate that allowed people to pass in or out, and some of the larger fences could be swung open or closed. There was a fence like this on Saint Street, the utility road. The large Saint Street gate swung open or closed across the road, allowing cars to pass from one side of campus to the other. At the end of the fence was a smaller gate, wide enough for just one or two people to pass at a time.

"The first lick was thrown right by my gate," said the campus aide assigned to the Saint Street gate. Outfitted with no more than a radio and a yellow security windbreaker, she radioed for support and closed the gate—standard procedure to prevent the spread of fighting and to keep some semblance of control over the movement of students. Usually it worked—but not this time. Some kids hopped the fence to join in the fighting. Others begged to be let through the gate and away from the action. It was 1:00 P.M.

Officers Palacio and Terry watched three boys launch into a full-on fistfight with three others—and started to head over to break it up. But then Palacio noticed that a much larger group of black kids was gathering on one side of the quad, and Latino kids were grouping on the other. Kids were separating from each other by race. The only thing that kept them apart were the thorny rose bushes in the middle of the quad.

"Oh, shit," Palacio said. "This is about to be a race riot."

He called on his radio for additional units to come to the school, and school administrators put the school on lockdown, which meant that teachers kept their students in their classrooms and all the gates were closed. In theory, the campus was sealed. But it was too little, too late. There were no more than a dozen adults at hand—aides and administrators—and hundreds of students. Making matters worse, there was no real way of knowing who was a student and who might be an adult or youth from another school. Locke was officially a closed campus, but students and others often snuck over the fences if they wanted to go to one of the nearby burger or taco joints. "There was grown men here," said a sophomore who witnessed the fighting. "Grown men all in white T-shirts."

Aides and administrators tried to make a human wall between the two groups, hoping to block or at least delay any physical confrontation, but kids kept ducking under and squirming through to get at each other. By the time Palacio looked up again, there were "seventy-five guys fighting with seventy-five other guys, big clusters of boys wrestling and swinging at each other not just on Saint Street but also in other parts of the quad."

"It just went like a fire," said the aide posted at the gate, who could see it all happening in front of her.

Another football player named Kerón was in the middle of it all. He had been walking his girlfriend back to class when he heard a commotion going on behind him. The sophomore wasn't going to bother with it, but then he saw his friend Anthony surrounded by Latino boys.

"I seen just a pile, fists, swinging," said Kerón. "I told Anthony his nose was bleeding. Then I turned around and said, 'Everybody hit somebody.' And they did."

"I ain't never seen anything like that in my life," he said. "It was like a thousand people fighting. It was everywhere."

Of course it wasn't quite that large, and the vast majority of Locke students were bystanders or victims who watched what was happening and tried to find someplace safe. Most of the students had no interest in fighting. Kids were screaming and running, hiding for safety behind any adult they could find, climbing fences and trees to get away from being hurt. Some kids hid in the covered eating area, watching from behind the gates. Others took refuge in the bungalows—the trailers used as classrooms that bookended the quad. Some kids waited for someone to swing at them.

But the scene was still total madness. A small black boy pounded on a bigger Latino boy who had challenged him. Other boys jumped in to protect their friends. Large boys hit and kicked much smaller girls. One student was surrounded by a group of black boys and beaten by the group. Most of the time, no one cared whom they hit; they were just swinging at whomever they could find who was of the opposite race. Then even more kids started running toward the fight.

"It seemed like people were hitting each other at random," said a sophomore honors student, who was sitting with a friend at the opposite corner of the quad. "If you got hit, you hit back." She tried to run back to class, located on the other side of campus, only to be turned back. The gates were blocked; the doors to the school were locked. There was nowhere to go.

The fighting went back and forth, repeatedly stopping and then starting up again. A small Latino boy named Ricky, was heading to class when a black kid cracked him on the jaw. For a few minutes he went crazy, swinging at every black kid he saw.

The adults tried to help until one of the administrators got himself caught up in the middle of a fight and had to be rescued by the police officers, who told him to back off. They were all supposed to wait rather than wade in; a school police officer had been punched and kicked in the head during a similar incident at a nearby high school just a few years before, and students had gotten close to getting control of an officer's handgun during another recent incident. But they were unable to stand by and watch kids getting beaten down by groups of other kids—especially when boys started attacking girls and ganging up on isolated kids. Officer Terry stepped in to try to break up mismatched situations, running after different fighters. "You would try to stop this one and another would break out," he said. "It was like trying to plug a hole in a dam."

Palacio followed behind, yelling at his partner, "We can't help them, we can't help them." Finally, he was able to get Terry to stop. They'd called dispatch, and they knew from the sound of the sirens that backup was coming. They just had to wait. While they did, the fighting continued in fits and starts. Groups of black and Latino boys circled the quad and jumped in on kids of the opposite race. They'd throw a few punches, then resume circling. It felt as though it had been going on forever, but in reality, just a half hour had passed.

Palacio came up with the idea of splitting the kids into two different parts of the campus—blacks in the auditorium where the dance had just been held, Hispanics in the gym. He didn't know if it would work; Locke kids weren't usually very cooperative when asked to follow shouted instructions. But he couldn't stand by, and he couldn't think of anything else, so he told the administrators and aides to start herding kids away from the quad.

Back in the main building, administrators hoped to keep kids from coming into the maze of halls, bathrooms, and classrooms. Up on the second floor of the main building, math teacher Zeus Cubias was eating lunch and working with students. He paid little attention to lockdown announcements. They'd become so common that they weren't worrisome anymore. English teacher Bruce Smith felt much the same way. Below a certain decibel level, shouting and screaming wasn't all that unusual.

Meantime, the sound of sirens grew increasingly loud. Math teacher Fernando Avila was driving back from an off-campus meeting when he saw squad cars speed by. *I hope they aren't going to Locke*, he thought to himself. Finally, reinforcements started to arrive from the parking lot and through the main gate. They put on black helmets with clear plastic face shields, batons and pepper spray at the ready. Some wore blue windbreakers; others had on short-sleeved shirts.

English teacher Kevin Sully went into colleague Joshua Beardall's room to watch from the window onto Saint Street as more and more police arrived below. Lockdowns were nothing new at Locke, but riot police were something relatively unusual. They had been there almost exactly a year before, in the aftermath of the dismissal of former principal Frank Wells, who had been removed for supporting the Green Dot takeover of the school. They were also there in 2003, lining up in the parking lot at San Pedro and marching in through the gate on Saint Street with batons and face masks, just as they were about to do now.

Still, neither teachers nor the two officers on campus had ever seen so many police gathered in one place. In all, more than one hundred officers from a variety of law enforcement agencies responded. The school police department sent its command post vehicle and set up a temporary headquarters at the day-care center across the street. It seemed as though the whole police department was there.

Once assembled, the officers formed skirmish lines—groups of ten or twelve—to go into the quad and try to restore order.

Soon after the fighting began, word began to spread among parents and in the neighborhood that Locke was on lockdown and that riot police were on their way. It started with a confused phone call from a student to a parent. And then another, and another. Within minutes, concerned parents had begun arriving at the school. They found the front gate, as well as the other gates, all locked, but there was no one to talk to them. Confusion grew. Rumors spread. They pressed against the gates, demanding to see their children. Students crowded at the windows and tried to communicate what little they knew to parents outside. The lights in the hallways were off, making the school seem dark and deserted even though the kids, teachers, and staff were in classrooms, the gymnasium, and the auditorium.

Parents at the front gate begged to be able to retrieve their children. But no one was allowed to leave, and there was no official news about what was happening inside.

News about the fighting was starting to get out to Green Dot, too. Founder Steve Barr got the word in his downtown office, jumped into his car, and headed down the freeway toward the school. Principal-in-waiting Coleman was already on her way to Locke when she looked up and saw helicopters circling in the sky, some from the LAPD, others from local TV news stations. When she arrived, her way was blocked by a slew of police cars and TV camera vans with their satellite antennae extended into the sky. A row of TV reporters stood in line in front of the school, each talking into a camera. *What have I taken on?* thought Coleman as she drove home.

Most of the kids dispersed when the police appeared in their riot gear. Once the fighting was quelled and the kids were contained in various locations around the school, the next issue was to figure out how to get everyone out of the school and back home safely. If they let everyone go at the same time, the fighting could easily resume on the streets. The solution was to release students in small groups. The process began at 2:30. Last to be released were the students separated into the gym and the auditorium. Officers suspected these two groups of having started the fighting, and wanted them to be last to go.

By 5:00 it was all over.

The public might be forgiven for thinking that school riots take place all the time. Those that do take place generate tremendous press coverage and public condemnation. That night, the image of riot police marching across the quad at Locke played on cable news shows across the nation. But school riots aren't in fact all that common, and many members of the Locke community bitterly resented the use of the term. Though it was reported afterwards that six hundred students had been involved, nearly everyone discounted that figure almost immediately. "If there were 600 people involved, 15 were fighting and 585 were watching," quipped one student. No tasers were used, no gunshots were fired, and no one was seriously injured. Four people were treated for minor injuries. Three students (and one nonstudent) were arrested. "Do anybody know what a riot *is*?" asked a student. "A riot is Rodney King. A riot is where stuff is burning, at least. Somebody's going to get killed in a riot."

Whatever name it went by, it was still a sad, scary end to a long, difficult year. Unfair as the coverage was, the violence that took place that day would define Locke for a long while. The next day of school, reporters and television cameras were at the campus before the start of class, asking students and teachers about the experience and—it seemed—waiting to see if any fighting would break out again.

PART TWO

..

"NEW" LOCKE

7

"NEW" LOCKE

Just before 8:00 A.M., a stream of teenagers flowed down San Pedro Avenue, the big street running up and down the west side of Locke's massive campus. Off the bus, out of parents' cars, or on foot, the flow of students grew denser the closer it came to the front gate of the school. Some of them seemed too small and young to be in high school. Others seemed impossibly large and adult. Most came by foot.

From San Pedro, the students turned onto 111th Street, a quiet one-way side street with a day-care center and a row of small ranch-style homes on its south side. On the north side stood the fence surrounding Locke, whose campus took up two full blocks, stretching all the way down 111th to Avalon Boulevard. The line of fences was broken up only occasionally by baby-blue-painted buildings and entranceways. The main building loomed three stories over the entrance, tall, concrete cinder block painted baby blue.

The stream of students passed the faculty parking lot, the school's electric marquee and a massive silver flagpole, a couple of police squad cars and TV news trucks parked in front of the school, and finally reached the front gate. There at the narrowing opening they bunched tighter to pass into the school.

Not all of the arriving students were allowed to go straight inside, however. Several—almost all of them boys—stood in little clusters off to both sides of the front gate unbuckling their belts and shoving the tails of their shirts down into khaki pants. Some put their bags and folders down on the pavement to get the job done. Some handed their backpacks to a friend. Others tried to pull off the awkward maneuver with one hand. Many glanced around to see if anyone was watching this partial public undressing. Once inside, they tugged their shirts and rearranged their belongings like airline travelers after going through security.

This year, for the first time ever, Locke teenagers long used to wearing pretty much anything they wanted—flip-flops (or, as the kids called them, slippers), jeans that sagged low below the hipbones, do-rags, cutoff sleeves, halter tops, gang colors, and white T-shirts that went down to the knees—were suddenly required to wear school uniforms and to keep their shirts tucked in while on campus. Print reporters and TV news camera crews were watching closely to see if kids would actually comply.

Helping make sure everyone was ready to enter, rookie principal Ronnie Coleman stood out on the sidewalk in a pantsuit and blouse, megaphone hung over her shoulder, reminding students about the new requirements as they walked by. Friendly and firm, the fast-moving Coleman caught nearly everyone who wasn't dressed right. A few feet behind her stood Green Dot founder Steve Barr, tall and imposing with a shock of white hair, shaking hands with some students and calling out the handful who had passed Coleman and still had their shirttails out. "Come on, handsome, get that thing tucked in," said Barr to a thin boy who tried to ignore him. "If I can do this, so can you."

Farther down 111th Street at another entrance, rookie assistant principal Zeus Cubias greeted students in much the same way. "Mi hijo," the former math teacher said to one of the many kids who greeted him warmly. "You know what to do. Don't even make me tell you."

Now thirty-four, Cubias had been tapped by Coleman to oversee roughly half of the returning Locke students. He had long, wavy brown hair, small hoop earrings in each ear, a closely trimmed goatee, and chunky glasses. A tattoo peeked out from under his short-sleeved shirt. A tiny microphone was perched on his lapel, courtesy of the camera crew from *Nightline* following his every move.

It was September 8, 2008, the first day of the first year of the "new" Locke. The school had been in bad shape in 2007 when Green Dot won approval to take it over and even worse shape by the end of the 2007–2008 school year when Green Dot finally took the reins. But now, forty-one years after the school had first opened its doors, the new Locke was finally open for business. It was, as promised, a new school. New management. New rules. New teachers. New everything. Everyone was getting a fresh start.

A few determined boys tried to get into school without tucking in their shirts, sliding past the adults, hiding behind their friends, or simply ignoring the instructions they were given. A couple tried outright defiance. "Fuck if I'm going to tuck my shirt in for you," spat one black-shirted boy, pushing his way into the school and disappearing up the wide stairway into a mass of students heading to class. Veteran campus aide Mike Lamb took off after him and returned a few minutes later with a tight smile on his face and one hand firmly latched on to the offending student's collar. The message was clear: this uniform thing was no joke. Kids couldn't go ten feet without being asked to take off their hats, asked where they were supposed to be, herded back inside the building, and—most confusing of all—thanked for being in uniform. The few kids who were out of uniform were stopped, asked politely but firmly to tuck in their shirts or to go home or to the uniform loaner room and borrow a uniform shirt if they needed one, and stopped again as many times as necessary. Security guards at one of the gates stopped a kid for wearing a button-down dress shirt instead of a polo shirt. He was out of uniform, too.

Under the new rules, everyone attending Locke had to wear tan pants and a collared shirt. The uniform was intended to make it easy to identify Locke students and make a break from the past. The tuck-in requirement was there to prevent the baggy-shirted gangbanger look. Before school started, there had been some uncertainty about whether or not the requirements would actually be enforced. Locke students were used to rules being announced and promptly forgotten. Some staff—including Cubias—thought the uniform requirement was unnecessary or even dehumanizing. But they had agreed that they needed to stand together and knew that if they didn't enforce the uniform rules right from the start, those rules—and many of their other changes—might not last for long. Arbitrary as it was, the uniform requirement was a make-or-break issue. They would be telling kids to tuck in their shirts every day for the rest of the year, and they knew it. They all kept telling themselves that it would be a full year before the kids got used to the new situation.

"It could have been anything," said veteran Locke math teacher Fernando Avila, who supported the change to Green Dot. "Long-sleeved shirts, whatever. They just have to enforce something."

●●

Once inside the front gate, students entered a long, shadowy breezeway, a cool tunnel running the full length of the building. To the left was the old principal's office (now renamed the

Welcome Center). To the right stood four yellow doors going into the three-story main building that would house "Big" Locke. Under Green Dot's plan, Locke had been divided into five different schools, all sharing the same campus. Each had it own schedule, entrances, and teachers. Each had its own budget and annual school rating, and each principal hired his or her own staff. Three of the new schools on campus were small—"baby" Lockes, as many teachers started calling them almost immediately. They served only incoming freshmen. The fourth—Locke 4—was a small alternative program for kids who were seriously behind on credits or were former dropouts or had been incarcerated. Last but not least there was Big Locke, which would serve all of the older students on campus—sophomores, juniors, and seniors who had gone to Locke in the past. These were the legacy kids—or the "transition" students, as Green Dot sometimes called them—the kids whom veteran Locke teachers were concerned for, the kids they'd stayed on to teach.

Big Locke was divided up into two halves, one with white uniform shirts and the other with black. The black-shirted students (aka the "black shirts" or the "black side") got the south side of the main building; the white shirts got the north side. Except for a weekly shared lunch, a handful of electives, and after-school activities like sports and clubs, the black shirts were kept apart from the white shirts and vice versa. The black shirts were made up of roughly eight hundred returning Locke students, including many of the football team, all of the kids learning English (about two hundred of them), and most of those identified as having special education needs. It also included more than a dozen kids who had to sign into school each morning for their parole officers, a handful who wore ankle bracelets monitoring their whereabouts, and several kids like Kerón and Anthony and Ricky who had been involved in the melee last spring. Cubias was in charge of them all.

Coleman had surprised some observers when she picked Cubias to head the black shirts. His new spot was one of the top jobs on campus, and he was the only veteran Locke teacher hired for an administrative position. "You sure you want this guy on board?" one colleague had asked Coleman. "I'm still waiting on grades from him from first semester." But Cubias was that rarest of birds: a Locke alumnus who had graduated, gone on to a four-year college, and returned to the community as a professional. He knew every nook and cranny of the campus and many of the parents of kids currently attending Locke. He got along with nearly everybody—black, white, and Latino—and he was passionate about the kids and the school. "I needed that energy—someone to build school culture," said Coleman. Making sure Big Locke had a strong sense of community was particularly important because the school contained the older kids who'd been through the wringer in recent years and also because Big Locke was going to be shrinking every year.

The eldest son of El Salvadoran immigrants, Cubias had grown up near the school when it was still mostly black, attended the local elementary schools that Locke kids still came from now, graduated from Locke in the early 1990s, and married his high school sweetheart, another Locke graduate (though they had since divorced). He spoke of his childhood fondly, though it was not without tragedy. When he was sixteen, his cousin Spanky was shot dead around the corner from Cubias's home. When he was a senior, the Rodney King riots erupted nearby.

Cubias hadn't been an early Green Dot enthusiast, and for a time he'd thought he might have to leave Locke once Green Dot took over. But he was committed to Locke, and he liked Green Dot enough to have sent his son to one of their schools for freshman year. Just as important, Cubias couldn't imagine working for a "normal" district school with a straitlaced principal—and if Green Dot "fixed" Locke he would be sad not to have helped make sure that they did it right. There was a challenge there, an excitement that was hard to resist, even though Cubias was unsure of his leadership skills and ambivalent about leaving the classroom. When Coleman asked him if he wanted to be one of the point men in charge of the biggest group of older Locke kids, Cubias agreed to stay—for the kids, if not for Green Dot.

"My work here is not done," he said. "This place gave me my two kids. It is who I am. This is the community. This is me."

The year before, well before his new position had been announced, Cubias arrived at a party showing off a freshly inked tattoo—his first. Wrapped in cellophane, the tattoo had been done in a converted garage by a Peruvian guy who was the brother-in-law of a recent acquaintance. A couple of shots of rum helped calm Cubias's nerves and deaden the pain, but now the tattoo was starting to hurt like hell. For a while, Cubias had thought about getting the El Salvadoran flag, symbol of his ancestral home. But he also liked the image of the Watts Towers, a tall sculpture made of wire and ceramic that pierced the low-slung neighborhood skyline and resembled church spires; no one could ever believe that the Towers were part of Watts. And, although Cubias wasn't religious in the formal sense, the idea of redemption was a powerful one for him. He was supposed to keep the tattoo covered to prevent infection, but once at the party he couldn't resist showing it off to his friends. There, inked in black on his right bicep was the image of Christ the Redeemer superimposed over the Watts Towers. Every one of his friends who saw it knew instantly that it meant Cubias had decided to stay at Locke and become part of the new school.

••

Partly because of Cubias, and partly because of its location close to the main gate, the black side of Big Locke would become the public face of the "new" Locke; it was the first place anyone saw or visited, the subject of the brunt of the media attention. Cubias was the person reporters were sent to talk to. Coleman might be in charge of Big Locke, but it was Cubias' school. He was colorful, friendly, and a refreshing mix of glib and sincere around colleagues, students, and outsiders alike. Every morning he zipped into the parking lot in the dusty blue minivan he jokingly called the Pussy Magnet. Then he scuttled down the path toward the school, leather briefcase in one hand, a giant cup of coffee in the other, and a lanyard with a janitor-sized clump of keys hanging from around his neck. All day long, he scurried around the halls, rounding up students, heading off trouble, and resolving minor conflicts. Always on the go, Cubias usually opened locked doors without taking his lanyard off his neck, instead bending forward with his face dangerously close to the doorknob. (He prided himself on having nearly every key there was to have.)

During crowded break or lunch periods, he sometimes got lost in the crowds of noisy, oversized teenagers, but you could always hear the big booming voice he used to banter with the kids: "Afuera!" Cubias told the kids who lingered in the hallways during lunchtime, reluctant to go outside. "You're just wasting my time," he told Ricky, who was wearing his uniform untucked and his pants too low. Cubias played at locking a girl in the bathroom, and then blocked some kids who tried to reenter the hallway. He wagged his finger in front of his face when they made excuses about not being in uniform. "Someone hold my earrings," he said, pretending to get ready to fight with some girls who were in a heated argument, distracting everyone long enough for the tension to dissipate. Kids who asked for lunch money got the standard response: "I already paid my child support this month." In between encounters, he hummed to himself and surveyed the crowd.

The kids weren't shy about giving it back to Cubias. "I'm still at the part where they made you vice principal," said one boy during lunch. "You only two feet tall—you ain't no pimp." And it wasn't just the kids. "Cubias is the worst kid in your school," said Cubias's counterpart Charles Boulden, head of the white side. Cubias's coworkers called him "Hollywood" for his stylish dress and his frequent media appearances. He preferred "the Snake Charmer," a name given to him by a former colleague on account of his legendary powers of persuasion. With Cubias, everyone got a nickname. Coleman was "Ronisha." Dean of Students Mike Moody was "Reverend" or "the Tooth Chipper." Guidance Counselor Emily Kaplowitz was "Em-i-ly" (strung out into three long syllables). He converted some of the black boys' names into Spanish and called some of the Latino skateboarders his "snakes." (They called him "snitch.") Everyone else just called him some variation on his last name: "Kobe" or "Koob" or "Cube."

He shook hands with everyone, over and over again, all day, every day. At a certain point the ritual handshaking and fist-bumping became sort of talismanic. Cubias was the kids' good luck charm, or vice versa.

"I love this place," he said one day early on, standing in the quad looking out over the kids during lunch—his favorite time of the day. "I love being here." He was always on campus. He hated to leave even for a moment. He wanted to get married at the school—if and when he was ready to get married again.

The only thing Cubias didn't like about his new job was the constant stream of meetings. They were wastes of time to him, a dangerous distraction from what was going on in the halls and classrooms he constantly patrolled. The only thing Cubias didn't like about the "new" Locke was how much more white the new Locke faculty had become despite all efforts to recruit minorities. A longtime critic of alternative training programs like Teach For America (TFA), he said, "I hate those Hollywood movies about when the middle-class white girl comes in and saves the poor kids." About Green Dot, there was a whole host of things Cubias didn't like—the uniforms, the lengthy double class periods, and especially the armed security guards and the black tarps that had been attached to many of the chain-link fences on campus. Intended to divide Locke into separate schools and protect students from being harassed or attacked from anyone on the surrounding streets, the tarps made the school like some sort of Gothic construction zone or a Cristo-style public art installation. (They were perceived by some students as walling the school off, as if Green Dot was ashamed of Locke kids or had something to hide.) But Cubias was willing to go with those things if it meant making Locke better. Green Dot was the lesser of two evils.

"This was a place that was just utterly ignored, ignored at every level," said Cubias in a *Nightline* interview. "We might as well call it Atlantis." He hoped that the past mistreatment was going to end and that Locke students would shine as they never had before. He wanted everyone to know that the old Locke wasn't the real Locke. "No man, that's not what we are."

And if there ever were a movie version of the Locke turn-around story, which he hoped there would be, Cubias said he wanted Johnny Depp to play him.

8

STRAY DOGS IN THE QUAD

Once the kids were settled in the first period of class, teachers explained the new rules and procedures and did their best to establish themselves as the ones in charge.

"You know how it was last year?" English teacher Monica Stone asked a classroom full of sophomores on the first day. The kids nodded and smiled at the young teacher. "Well, it's gonna be different this year," said Stone, hoop earrings swinging as she turned to give everyone in the room as serious a look as she could muster. She and other teachers emphasized that whatever experiences students may have had in the past in school, at the new Locke, teachers cared about their students, wanted to help them pass their classes, and would not abandon that effort. "I'm going to shake your hand every day no matter what," Stone said. "Don't worry about germs—I've got lots of hand sanitizer."

Giving up on school was the worst problem for the Locke kids. Teachers said that they tended to give up at the slightest obstacle, overreacting to a failed quiz or missed homework or a difficult question in class. And they tended to give up for a long time. Then they failed. And then they dropped out. It was a steep and slippery slope, and Locke teachers knew they had to watch carefully for the first signs of disengagement. Some gave easy little quizzes about class procedures during those first few days, largely as a way to encourage kids to see that they could succeed.

"I don't play favorites, and I don't hold grudges. I am here to help you," said Olympia McNutt, slowly walking around her classroom as students filled out forms about what they wanted to get out of the school year. "I will never ask you to do anything that harms you," said McNutt, whom almost everyone called Miss Olympia. "Therefore I need you to do what I ask."

Some teachers also took time to explain a little bit about how Locke was being run by Green Dot this year instead of the school district. Green Dot had invited a group of Locke students to visit a Green Dot school the previous spring, and posted several videos of kids and parents talking about how great Green Dot was. But it still was hard for many students to grasp exactly what was going on besides all the new rules. Some kids called Green Dot the "new owners," as if the school were a baseball team.

There was also lot of playacting between teachers and students, some of whom liked to act tough just to see if they could get a reaction from teachers.

"Watch it," said one student to her new teacher. "I pushed my last teacher down the stairs."

"I'm from El Salvador," responded the teacher, with an arched eyebrow and a mock scowl. "You mess with me and your whole family is dooooomed."

One thing was clear right from the start: Locke students were keenly aware of being noticed by adults, and remarkably responsive to adults they perceived to be caring and supportive. "They don't care what you know until they know you care," said Kaplowitz, the new counselor who had worked tirelessly to sort out transcript snafus and get students scheduled into classes they needed. The importance of caring and relationships over content or anything else was a mantra repeated by many of the adults on campus. And showing you cared didn't take all that much, according to Kaplowitz. "All you have to do is remember their names."

Kaplowitz and many of the teachers weren't immediately warm and welcoming with the kids, however. In fact, there was a flat, blank, "Why should I care?" look that many of the adults on campus seemed to have perfected for use instead of a smile that might be used in another situation. Teachers would hold this flat stare for a moment, then give a smile or a bit of praise. The ritual seemed like a check against being taken for granted or being thought of as a pushover—or maybe just a disguise for youth and inexperience.

By and large, the kids were quiet and observant during the first few days and weeks. They were still getting a feel for things, and often didn't know many other kids in the classes to which they'd been assigned. Their friends were in other classes or even other schools. They were waiting to see if this new set of faces—if Green Dot—really meant to follow through on its promises of a quality education.

••

In the halls and walkways outside of class, the school was remarkably quiet. The hallways were freshly painted the same light blue as the outside of the building. The linoleum floors were clean and brightly polished. The double-wide stairways going up to the second and third floors were free of graffiti. The only sounds were the occasional slam of a classroom door, the kerthunk of the big pushbar doors leading out onto the quad, the thwap of a rubber doorstop being flipped up, and the low crackle of the radios administrators and security used to keep in touch with each other.

In stark contrast to the past, there weren't any of the so-called "walkers" wandering around the halls and open spaces of the school. "Even if you sneak out of class, there's no one to talk to," said one student during the first few days. "It's weird. I don't like it." Locke was "boring" now, the kids complained. "It irks me, but it's helping," said one junior about all the new procedures and rules.

On the first floor, dean of students Mike Moody chatted with teachers passing by on their way to the copy room and checked that students headed to the bathroom had hall passes. On the second floor, Coach Vic Lopez, a campus aide and football coach, sat halfway down the hallway in a small blue chair, reading a paperback. On the third floor, longtime campus aide Mike Lamb was going through culture shock just as much as the students. He was used to a regular stream of students and disturbances to make the days go quickly, but now the halls were mostly empty, and the students weren't mouthing off the way he was used to.

"I need a fight," said Lamb, looking around his empty third-floor hallway and smacking an elbow against the palm of his opposite hand, giving his trademark bug-eyed "Psycho" stare. But Lamb wouldn't get his wish—at least not on the first few days of school. "Did you hear about the big fight today?" Coleman asked her colleagues three days into the first week. "No? Well that's because there wasn't one." The joke delighted Coleman enough to use it several more times in succession. Indeed, the students Coleman talked to spoke about how surprised and delighted they were that their teachers cared about them, were on them to do homework when no one else had been in the past. The kids were hungry for change, Coleman said, and appreciative of being treated decently. At an assembly held at the end of the first week, they hooted and applauded for their new teachers and administrators—something many doubted would have happened in the past. Teachers and staff, most of them strangers just a few weeks ago, quickly began to form friendships and cohesiveness. "People are amazed at the school," said Coleman. "They're just astounded."

Coleman was particularly happy to discover that many of the office staff Green Dot had agreed to hire from the district turned out to be unexpectedly helpful. Ms. Burnett, Coleman's clerk, was knowledgeable about things that no one else on campus seemed to know about—from simple matters like how to get the mail delivered to more complex issues like how to get information from the district. She made sure that Coleman looked at mail that needed attention and didn't miss any key deadlines. She could find anything Coleman needed, and she had keys to get into almost as many different rooms as Cubias.

"There were a lot of little things she caught that could have caused a *big* mess," said Coleman. Through a process that remains somewhat disputed Burnett got the fancy title of "cluster leader." "I don't complain," said Coleman. "She can call herself whatever she wants."

For their part, clerks and aides and office workers appreciated being treated like part of the team. In the past—at most schools—nonteachers weren't usually invited to staff retreats or training sessions, or encouraged to speak up at staff meetings. All that was different now, and it made a tremendous difference in emotional and practical terms. For the first time, clerks and campus aides knew if someone walking by was a teacher or not. In the past, they'd had no real opportunity to get to know the faculty. Coleman and other administrators regularly asked for—and took—ideas from anyone who had them, including Lopez and Lamb and Burnett.

"There's light-years of difference," said Fred Lee, a Locke graduate and campus aide who worked at one of the baby Lockes on the other side of campus. "We were on our own before. Now we've come together."

••

Over the first few weeks, it seemed as if the positive energy and goodwill were contagious. Teachers had classrooms, by and large. Kids had schedules, by and large. Daily attendance was up—almost 90 percent if the numbers were to be believed. The adults were showing up and going where they were supposed to go. Students and parents reported that they felt safe at the school and that their teachers cared about them. There was momentum and enthusiasm surrounding the start of the new school, the belief—part hope, part confidence—that they could really turn Locke around. Slowly, the kids settled into their new roles and got used to the new rules and procedures. "What side are you on?" students playing on a sports team might ask each other. The appropriate response: "the white shirts" (or "the white side"). Late students knew that they had to wait to get into class rather than walk in one by one. There were no more than a handful of isolated fights—small, one-on-one scuffles that were squashed almost immediately. The separation into different schools was strange and new, along with the new schedule and longer class periods and uniforms, but ditching and tardiness were down. Teachers still wrote students up for classroom defiance, but nothing close to a group brawl even took shape. Over eight hundred parents showed up for back-to-school night, which had been nearly abandoned in the past. "I never had more than eight parents show up, and last night I had over fifty," said English teacher Maggie Bushek. "It was extremely cool."

What made the momentum and enthusiasm all the more unlikely was a series of problems that had emerged over the

summer and remained unresolved even after the doors opened
for the start of the year. Green Dot failed to anticipate that the
district might be unable or unwilling to provide electronic access
to student transcripts over the summer, creating confusion and
uncertainty about scheduling kids so that they would meet the
state graduation requirements. Started late and interrupted by
the riot, the hiring of teachers just never got finished. A handful
of classes were being taught by unqualified substitutes. Then,
at an overnight retreat held about a week before school opened,
things got out of hand when Coleman, Cubias, and Boulden
came up with the very bad idea of playing a drinking game
they called "Shots with a Principal," which proved so popular
that pretty much the entire staff ended up drunk out of their
minds—an experiment Coleman regretted immediately (but
others felt bonded the new team together).

Even after school started, the list of problems remained so
long that it was hard to imagine how the school kept running every day. Books hadn't arrived yet. The bells didn't work
properly. Nearly a quarter of the kids were coming late to
school—hundreds each day. The phones didn't function reliably. Staff and guards couldn't hear each other on their two-way
radios. The class schedule was so complicated that students were
often confused about where to go. There was a ten-minute
break between morning classes labeled "snack" on the schedule,
but—for the first day or two—nothing for kids to eat.

"Who takes over a problematic high school in Watts and
puts a brand-new principal and two brand-new APs in charge?"
asked English teacher Kevin Sully, one of the youngest (and most
persistently skeptical) Locke veterans. He derided the new team
as a "junior varsity squad for a varsity game."

Yet it all seemed to be working out. Mistakes that came
up seemed small and were quickly rectified. The kids lobbied

successfully for a rooter bus for a big away football game. After-school clubs and student activities were brought back, along with new electives like philosophy and journalism. The yearbook and the school paper were also brought back. Lobbied by students, administrators decided to allow skateboarding in the quad after school. Now the students just had to arrive at school on time and in uniform, go to class, do their class work, and try not to swear as much. That would come in time, everyone seemed to agree. Meanwhile, the kids generally seemed willing to tolerate the rules if the other changes—a safe environment and caring teachers—became reality. Green Dot couldn't change these kids' home circumstances, but maybe it could change their life chances.

••

The transformation of the quad was perhaps the biggest change of all to the campus. Over the weekend before classes started, twenty new trees had been planted around the quad, along with row after row of dark green grass that was so new that yellow tape was set up around the perimeter to give it more time to take root. The new trees and the renovation of the quad were a last-minute donation from actress Cameron Diaz, who had heard about the Locke transformation and wanted to come talk to Barr about helping out. Barr had just returned from a meeting at Locke when Diaz arrived at Green Dot's downtown offices. "The quad looked like a prison yard to me," said Barr. "Asking her for trees was just the first thing that came to my mind."

Completely enclosed from the streets, the quad was now a leafy oasis in the middle of South Central LA. Jumbo jets flew high above, silently approaching Los Angeles International Airport. Birds chirped and the wind rustled through the leaves on the trees. The groundskeeper puttered around in his oversized straw hat. Most of the day, the quad sat empty and serene, making it hard to tell if there were even *any* students on campus. "Where are the kids?" visitors always asked. The quad came alive during lunch, when kids hurriedly ate and socialized. Some leaned against the wall or pressed themselves against their girlfriends or boyfriends or stood in a loose line of friends listening to music. Some signed up friends for clubs and field trips at tables lining one of the walkways. Cubias, Moody, Kaplowitz, and the rest of the staff stood at their supervision posts, chatting with kids and confiscating hats, finally herding students back into the big blue building for the second half of the day. After school, the Junior ROTC kids practiced their turns and marching on the walkways surrounding the grass. Skater kids did jumps and attempted tricks on the outdoor stage that stood next to the grass. "I am now an advocate of trees," said assistant principal Boulden, walking diagonally across the grass toward a meeting in the bungalows, with Cubias at his side.

Once it had been transformed, the quad became one of Barr's favorite places to visit when he was on campus. It was a convenient showpiece, a powerful visual symbol of the renewal he hoped to bring to the school. VIP tours inevitably lingered under the covered walkways that surround the well-manicured lawn. Barr even had a favorite shady corner where he liked to perch while talking to journalists. He was especially glad to see that the thorny rosebushes were gone from the center of the quad, both because they were scraggly and because they'd been installed to prevent large-scale fights rather than beautify the surroundings. "You know how you stop kids from fighting?" asked Barr, looking around the grassy quad a few days into the new school year. "You educate them." At one point later in the year, he would sit himself down cross-legged on the grass, trying to demonstrate to the kids that the grassy lawn wasn't just for show (and ignoring the dampness that came up from the wet grass).

For Barr, the opening of the new Locke was a dream fulfilled, a realization of Green Dot's larger mission. It had taken him almost four years to create the chance for Green Dot to try to do what everyone said couldn't be done—certainly not by noneducator like Barr and an untested charter school organization like Green Dot. But now Green Dot had over six hundred employees and seventy-two hundred students (and a small new satellite Green Dot in the South Bronx, the product of a fledgling partnership between Barr and teachers union president Randi Weingarten). It was finally all happening.

Barr's good mood had been growing since a couple of days before school started, when he had addressed the entire Green Dot organization gathered in the Locke gymnasium. Wearing jeans, an oversized polo shirt, and loosely laced tan work boots, Barr told them how fixing long-broken Locke was going to transform the entire city of Los Angeles.

> Imagine with me all the people that have attended Locke High School. Over forty years, that's about sixty thousand people that came to this school. Now imagine if you could get all these people all gathered in one place like Dodger Stadium. Imagine if you got on the public address system and said, "Those of you who did not graduate from Locke, please step out of the stadium." Forty thousand people would have to step out of that stadium. Now you'd have twenty thousand where there were sixty. Then if you got on the public address system and said, "All those who didn't get accepted to a four-year university, please step out." Now we're down to eight thousand people where there were once sixty thousand. Now you get on the public address system and say, "Please step out if you didn't get a college degree." All

but twenty-one hundred Locke Saints would have to leave that stadium. One section of it would be full. The rest of it would be empty seats. And if you asked those who remained, "How many of you came back to Watts?" the answer would be probably very few.

Then Barr asked the old Locke teachers to stand, and anyone who graduated from Locke, too. Among them was Cubias.

"When Locke happens, teachers and parents around this city will revolt," Barr said. "'I want *that*' is what they'll say. 'I want what Locke has.' And that's how we're going to change the city."

Out on the quad, only one massive tree remained from before Green Dot's arrival, a thick coral tree scarred from years of graffiti. Stray dogs, most of them small and scruffy, sometimes wandered through from the outside streets, looking for scraps of food and affection—no matter how hard the groundskeeper and others tried to keep them out.

9

IN THE CLASSROOM

In most ways, Locke kids were just like kids everywhere. Some of the girls wore elaborate outfits of matching boots and bags, along with tight pants and fancy hair accessories. Some of the boys brushed their hair so obsessively—back to front from the neckline to the forehead went the short-toothed brushes—that it seemed as if they might scrape their heads bald. Some kids wore oversized baseball caps that made their heads look shrunken. Other kids went the opposite direction, sporting tiny knit caps perched on the tops of their heads that gave them the look of a Dr. Seuss character. Earphones snuck out of shirts and from underneath hats, or when not in use hung over students' ears like towels on a rack. (One big kid even wore large clunky tan reading lab headphones instead of the usual tiny in-ear kind.) They claimed they could hear class discussion "just fine" with earphones in their ears or when their heads were down on their desks and their eyes were closed. They flicked their cell phones open at the end of class and turned their heads downwards, reading and texting madly. Hands together, heads bowed, buried in oversized hoodies, they looked as though they might be studying an obscure text written on a tiny piece of paper, prayerful monks walking down the halls.

They ate Flamin' Hot chips and drank Gatorade for breakfast and lunch. During the morning break, five or six kids sold junk food out of giant cargo bags unzipped in front of them on the floor. ("It's like a ghetto farmer's market out here," said one of the school clerks.) At lunch, they scarfed down the cafeteria food to leave more time for socializing or sports. A few students wandered the quad selling candies and chips out of their backpacks (including one particularly addictive, finger-staining brand of tortilla chip called Takis Fuego).

They were brash and mean and accepting all at the same time, constantly poking and prodding each other for weaknesses but rarely taunting kids who really couldn't read or who wore the same food-stained polo shirt to school day after day. They were boisterous, emotional, frequently hilarious. They had mood swings that made them friendly one day and hostile the next. They called adults they didn't know (or like) "Mister" or "Miss." (Some of the teachers thought it was nice—a cute alternative to "Hey, you," or "Teacher." Others thought it was impersonal and overly formal, alienating even.)

Locke classrooms were pretty normal, too, wide and deep with large windows and two doors. American flags hung off of wooden rods and student projects lined the back walls, stapled onto colored construction paper. The desks were the standard desk-chair combinations that looked much too small for many of the kids, with the wire rack underneath for books and supplies. The square white squawk box on the wall was immediately recognizable, though rarely used anymore. Tiny window frames in each door had been plated over with metal covers and rivets during a previous remodeling so that kids couldn't distract each other looking into class from the halls. Each room had old-fashioned wooden cabinets near the doorway, some left unlocked but others kept closed with bike chains.

Shiny whiteboards replaced green or black chalkboards, and LCD projectors replaced overhead transparencies. The teachers all had laptops, and a handful had fancy touch-screen whiteboards. But otherwise, classroom supplies remained largely unchanged from fifty years ago—stubby yellow pencils, cheap white binder paper and rough colored construction paper, spiral notebooks and clothbound composition books and three-ring binders. Three-ring binders, cheap black backpacks, and thin plastic ball-point pens remained the norm.

Even the structure of what went on during class was fairly normal. Teachers introduced lessons at the start of class; kids worked in groups or individually when they weren't doing a whole-class activity. Locke featured longer-than-usual blocks of time, rather than hourlong sessions common at many schools, but that was about it for change. Some teachers numbered tables or desks and assigned students to each spot. Others numbered individual chairs. Although it wasn't mandatory, nearly every class at Locke began with a warm-up activity of some kind: a brief introductory exercise each student did individually at his or her desk that was meant to settle and focus the kids. Others did individual reading activities at the end of class. A few showed video snippets from YouTube. There was no real Green Dot model when it came to classroom instruction, no "Green Dot way" of running a class or setting up the desks in a room. There weren't uniform practices or strategies being used across all the classrooms or among the different schools as with other, more regimented charter networks like KIPP.

To be fair, on most days what goes on in even the most successful classrooms isn't really all that exciting. Every experienced teacher has a showoff lesson or two, and every kid remembers a few fun moments or units he or she particularly liked, a semester or an elective that was particularly engaging. There's the occasional "fun" lesson, the occasional discussion where everyone participates, the rare "aha!" moment. And there are a handful of amazing teachers who make every day magical. But learning isn't always easy or comfortable or fun or even particularly linear. Grown-ups sometimes forget this, not having had to master a new skill or concept in a while. Successes are incremental. Progress is occasional. There's a tremendous amount of repetition. Learning accumulates slowly.

One of the first things you might notice about Locke kids was just how black and brown they were. It wasn't just that the school was 99 percent African American and Latino; there are lots of schools fitting that description. But Watts was geographically and culturally isolated from the rest of the city, and the longtime black families and newly arrived Latino families who sent their children to Locke didn't seem to have mixed. The faces you saw in the classrooms weren't like those of a typical TV sitcom where actors' features and skin tones are mixed together.

Visitors often thought that the school was still predominantly black, though that was no longer the case. In fact, the student body was two-thirds Latino. It was just that the black kids tended to be the loudest of the bunch—a matter of frequent joking. At times the noise was the cause of confusion for teachers who were unused to the high decibel level. They would sometimes kick students out of class for fighting when the kids were just engaged in loud conversation. In stark contrast, some of the Latino kids all but refused to talk in class or stood in a line against the wall during breaks, as though they were having some sort of unannounced silence contest, each trying to outlast the other. Of course, not everyone fit these stereotypes—there were plenty of quiet black kids and loud Latinos. The Latino kids weren't predominantly Spanish speakers, either; only about two hundred of them in the entire Big Locke population were in bilingual classrooms. For the majority of Latino kids, their parents and grandparents spoke Spanish, and they could chat and swear in Spanish, but that was about it.

Where Locke students really showed their differences was when they were called on to read something aloud or to write something down in class. During those activities, these kids who otherwise looked and acted just like average teenagers revealed academic foundations that were dishearteningly weak, the product of previous years of classroom learning that hadn't asked for or produced very much by way of literacy skills. This wasn't the case for every kid in every classroom—Locke had AP classes and electives where the work being done was more in line with what would be considered normal high school studies. Locke kids' smarts showed up all the time in how quickly they saw through the holes in teachers' logic, how articulately they described the despicable ways they'd been treated in previous schools, and how quickly they figured out how to game the lunch line. But there were several kids in most classes whom teachers knew not to ask to read aloud in front of their classmates, and many more whose ability to provide written responses was only at the grade school level. There were a handful of kids who were so far behind that they couldn't read a text message, who read like a second- or third-grader.

Compounding these academic deficiencies was the reality that, deliciously smart and insightful as they were, kids at Locke were no picnic to teach. In class, hulking boys and self-assured girls often acted like little kids—helpless, confused, overwhelmed, jokey, distracted by the smallest details, and incessantly goofing on each other. They interrupted, argued, didn't—couldn't—wait to respond. Or, just as challenging, they all but refused to do anything—talk in class, answer a question, write down an assignment.

It wasn't just the kids who were new to this kind of classroom, however. Coleman's teachers tended to be incredibly youthful and inexperienced—impossibly young TFA members who themselves looked like as if they might still be high school seniors (or at least TV actors playing high school students). Educators who know how to engage challenging kids to do rigorous work rarely take the form of inexperienced teachers—no matter how talented or full of potential they may be a few years down the line. It takes time to become an effective teacher, and even then not everyone can do it at an extremely high level of success. But fully half of the teachers in Big Locke were outright rookies. Seventy percent of the teachers had fewer than five years under their belts. A second-year teacher was a department head. A third-year teacher was a veteran. As a result, they didn't have a bag of tricks or proven lessons yet, and Green Dot hadn't given them any clear guidelines. "Unfortunately, a lot of what we did was trial and error," said one.

"I think maybe we're taking the 'green' part of the Green Dot name a bit too literally," said Cubias, bounding up the stairs to check on a third-floor classroom one morning. It was depressing to watch kids regress as soon as they stepped into the classroom, and disheartening to watch smart but inexperienced teachers stumble through lessons. The new Locke was being taught by twenty-somethings and run by thirty- and forty-somethings. There was very little grey hair to be seen during faculty meetings.

••

The lethargy and lack of momentum were especially noticeable in first-year teachers' classrooms, where time passed as slowly as in the slowest staff meeting you have ever been to, as slowly as you may remember time passing when you were a student. The lessons were long, the activities and transitions insufficiently engaging to jog students' attention. Copy it down. Answer these questions. Raise your hand if you think you know the answer. Teachers gave excruciatingly concrete instructions to students, telling them exactly where to put their pens and what to do. They explained how to take notes down to the tiniest detail, explaining how to copy more than one word at a time for greater copying speed. They herded kids along by talking almost nonstop, voices high and strained for fear of losing what little attention remained. Barely enough kids stayed involved that the conversation didn't fall apart entirely. The rest, bored out of their minds or lost, tried to amuse themselves. Some pushed their seats up against the back wall, balancing or bouncing. Others pulled their hoodies up over their heads and put their heads down on their desks, snuck headphones into their ears, or pulled out their cell phones and texted below the desk.

Lots of the teachers used point systems to keep things moving—points for having their books out, for participating, for group answers. "Ten points for you." The explicitness was intended to prevent confusion and make everyone feel that he or she could succeed in class, but made for extremely slow going and required compliance from students that sometimes seemed excessively strict. "This isn't Burger King," a teacher said to a student who wanted to take notes differently. "You can't have it your way." But the highly structured lessons and classroom rules were appalling to some of the newer teachers. "I don't want to resort to all these behavioristic techniques," said one young teacher sitting out in the quad after a long day in the classroom. "But the kids are saying things like, 'Miss, why don't you tell them to shut up?' And the [veteran] teachers here say you gotta do it."

Sometimes, the disruptions and cat herding began right at the start of class and never really ended. For example, one morning in January 2009, nearing the end of the first semester, sophomore Rhonda was among the last students to come into the classroom, wearing long shorts and a heavy jacket. The solidly built girl headed straight to her chair and slung her jacket over the back, then called out, "Does anybody have a pen I could borrow?"

"OOOOOO," went the high-pitched electronic tone that sounded like a kettle boiling over but actually marked the official beginning of class.

Pretty much everyone had his or her head down, writing out answers to the day's warm-up questions. Someone gave Rhonda something to write with, but it wasn't long before she was waving her hands and making goofy faces in the direction of a classroom visitor who was videotaping the lesson as part of an effort to help support new teachers. Rhonda's antics weren't anything serious—she just didn't want to settle down.

"Rhonda, that's one point," said the teacher from behind his desk at the front of the classroom. Almost immediately, Rhonda waved her hands and turned her head around to look at everyone again.

"Rhonda, that's two."

"What I'm doing, sir?"

"Rhonda, work on your warm-up."

Most teachers at Locke used some sort of classroom grading system to encourage participation and discourage disruptions. Lose too many points over the semester, and a student could receive a lower grade. Lose too many points in a single class period, and a student could get sent out of the room and down for a talk with Moody or Cubias.

A few minutes later, Rhonda got up and walked across the room, gesturing and mugging for the camera once more, with little attempt to hide what she was doing.

"Rhonda, that's three."

"I had to get one of these," said Rhonda, waving a few pieces of blank paper in her hand.

"Fine, but you know what you did," came the response.

Back in her seat, Rhonda waved her hands, made faces, and threw up hand signals again—not as enthusiastically as before, but her actions were clear. She wasn't going to give up that easily.

"Four, Rhonda."

The teacher got up from his desk and went over to Rhonda's chair, crouching down to talk to her. Approaching students individually and speaking to them quietly was another widely adopted strategy at Locke, intended to make things as private and nonconfrontational as possible. Or teachers would put a hand gently on the shoulders of students whose heads were already on their desks or who needed to settle down.

But by now, some of the other kids were acting up, talking to each other and poking their seatmates. Rhonda's antics were spreading.

"Please act normal," said the teacher, looking up and scanning the room.

"What's normal?"

"How you normally act," was the response. Then the teacher made a few announcements about upcoming tests and scheduling, turned the lights down, and cued up a video about teen dating violence.

In most cases, teachers tried to handle students like Rhonda on their own, keeping them after class, marking them down, or making them do extra work if they misbehaved. In a handful of cases, or where the disruptions were prolonged, teachers would open the classroom door and ask a student to stand outside the room or go downstairs to the office, hoping that there was a blue-shirted campus aide in the hallway as backup. Rhonda had already been sent down to the office numerous times. Sometimes she was mad about what had happened, but most of the time she seemed a little embarrassed by what she'd done. She'd give Cubias or Moody a goofy grin, and promise to do better controlling what she said and did. And then, a few days or weeks later, she'd mess up again.

••

It wasn't just in the beginners' classes where instruction was lacking. The best teaching at Locke was good, not great, and there wasn't enough of it. (The math department was considered particularly strong, including several Locke veterans with more than a handful of years in the classroom, and there was one stand-out bilingual education teacher who's teaching was particularly interesting, brisk, and engaging.) There wasn't much teaching that was outright awful, but that was about all that could be said. The teachers had all of them mastered difficult material. They knew what rigor was. But they didn't necessarily know how to *teach* it. And, like sleep-deprived parents who couldn't think straight, they couldn't see past the start of the next class. Many reverted back to their own classroom memories or to the most concrete, simplified approaches.

"I don't think our teachers are really ready for the 'rigor' thing this year," said Coleman, shaking her head after a particularly disheartening classroom observation in March.

In fact, most teachers did their best to help kids pass their classes. Locke teachers gave credit for every conceivable behavior—bringing materials to class, being ready when class started, copying information down from the board, helping collect materials or put things up on the board. In many Locke classrooms, kids had to work at failing. Not show up. Not participate in class. Not do *any* work or hand *anything* in. Not do any of the makeup work that was offered, or copy any notes off the whiteboard, or do anything to try to get any extra credit. Not write anything down on a quiz, even if you remembered the answer from the review the day before. Assuming the student showed up, it was harder to fail than to pass—and that was the goal. There were a hundred ways to pass.

"It's not hard to pass my class," said English teacher Amanda Esten, thumping her hand on the table for emphasis. "I let kids make up work. I give extra assignments."

Making classes easy to pass might seem like an awful thing to do, but it represented an understandable response to a difficult dilemma. Even the "regular" kids at Locke were many of them extremely behind in their writing and reading skills. They participated in class and did the work, but they weren't ready for anything rigorous. Their efforts were heartbreakingly rudimentary. What was better? Letting a kid pass a class in which he'd barely learned anything, in the hopes that he'd catch up later and benefit from having moved along, or flunking a kid and making him dig in at least a little bit, with the knowledge that such a thing might not happen? It was a difficult call—and an age-old question. Teachers—and schools—have been passing kids along for decades.

And still, the fail rate for core classes at the new Locke was over 40 percent. Kids weren't there, slept during class, and didn't hand in any work or even try to answer questions they might have gotten from memory or by accident. They slapped their backpacks down on the desk in front of them at the beginning of class and didn't move them for the next hour and a half, except perhaps to use them as pillows or bring them closer to conceal some in-class texting. They pulled out a spiral notebook from the wooden cabinet at the start of class, wrote a couple of things told to them, and put the binder back in the cabinet on the way out of the room at the end of the class, and that was it until two days later when the next class met. Most difficult of all, they tended not to see themselves as having any influence over their grades. The topic, or the teacher, overpowered their role. They only saw things happening to them.

"We're doing everything we can," said Barr. "But it's not our product. These kids are the product of eight years of neglect. Some of them have already been at Locke for three years. We've got seventeen-year-olds with no credits." It wasn't just academics that were holding them back either.

"There really are a lot of mental issues that plague our kids," said one of the administrators. "Grief and resistance, anger, bipolarism—the amount of mental and social emotional support that they need was not something that I would have known ahead of time."

10

SHOCKTOBER

First-year social studies teacher Jeremy Zuniga gulped from his water bottle and tried to get his history class to settle down.

"I don't need a bunch of people shouting out all at once," said Zuniga, his face a little shiny in the late-summer heat.

"Kick him out, Mister," said one of Zuniga's students, black-shirted sophomores, juniors, and seniors who needed the class to graduate.

"Yeah, kick him out," said a few others.

At Locke (as at most high schools), getting other students in trouble was a favorite pastime—especially toward the beginning of the year when kids didn't necessarily know each other but had begun to figure out that some of their teachers were uncertain about maintaining order. When the teacher was new and white and rumored to be gay but still in the closet, disrupting class was particularly tempting. Zuniga looked down at his notes and glanced around momentarily. There were almost forty-five minutes left in the class.

••

The first four weeks of the school year are a honeymoon period during which the kids are on their best behavior but also scoping out the weak links, looking for gaps and inconsistencies, plying teachers with sweetness. Now it was "Shocktober," the time period roughly coinciding with the month after which it is named, when, at nearly every school, pretty much everything—lesson planning, grades, problematic relationships, logistical bottlenecks—can come crashing down. Sometimes Shocktober is short, just a week or two until things get back into a good flow. Other times, it lasts well beyond into the following months. Veterans know it's coming, but Locke had precious few of those.

The long hundred-minute class periods were turning out to be particularly punishing. The longer classes were supposed to give kids more time to delve into what they were learning, to work on their own as well as in groups, and to limit the amount of time they spent moving from class to class every hour or so as they would in a normal school. But what, exactly, do you do as a rookie teacher in charge of high school students for more than an hour and a half? The longer periods also meant that classes met only every other day. By Wednesday, kids forgot what they'd been doing on Monday. A kid missing one day of class missed two days of material.

••

Zuniga survived the hundred-minute class through an improvised mixture of prodding and coaxing. Afterwards, he took the stairs from the second floor to the main office and asked for referral forms—paper slips teachers use to document student infractions—to document the behavior of students who'd refused to follow his instructions or cussed at each other (and at him). But, as far as Cubias and Moody could figure out, there weren't any such forms available. It would be a few more weeks before they were. Zuniga wrote down what had happened on a blank sheet of paper and returned to his classroom.

It wasn't just the long classes that made things different, and harder, for teachers. Now, under the new regime, there were even more colorful characters in teachers' classrooms— "knuckleheads," as some teachers liked to call them: kids who weren't used to sitting still, didn't want to be there, hadn't necessarily bought in to being in class and graduating from high school, and used to wander the halls or smoke under the bleachers.

"My mom says I should finish high school," said Manuel Borges, a sophomore on the black side who nearly always had a pencil behind his ear. "She wants me to be a policeman or something, but I just want to go to work."

All of these kids were now being pushed into classrooms by the aides and security guards. So were mildly disabled special education students, whom counselors had shifted into regular classrooms in an attempt to provide better services than they would get in a separate special education room.

"I thought I knew the Locke community," said one veteran teacher. "But I felt like it was my first year all over again."

They were working fourteen-hour days, waking up at 4:30, never having weekends, and—some of them—crying a lot. They were teaching materials they didn't know. They were exhausted from grading and preparing and dealing with students. They were photocopying chapters from books that hadn't arrived yet. They said they'd *never* use candy to get kids to participate and then found themselves going out and buying bags and bags of Now and Laters and M&M's. They knew they were letting kids fall through the cracks, but couldn't do anything about it. They were ignoring their friends and families. They got sick a lot. They thought about quitting.

"I wanted to crawl into fetal position and cry myself to sleep in the corner of my classroom," said one teacher. "I barfed up my breakfast into the sink, cried, and went to school," said another.

"I guess I didn't think I'd live past the first day," said Coleman, who called what was going on "organized chaos." She had dark circles under her eyes and found she had to use her reading glasses more and more. Then she developed back pain that got so bad she had to take a few days off work. Cubias was so rushed that he sometimes shaved and changed shirts in his office after the first period began. Problems came at him so fast and furious that he didn't bother writing anything down. There wasn't really time to handle anything but the most immediate crises. "This ain't no joke," said Cubias's counterpart Boulden, who by the end of October was well on his way to gaining twenty pounds and developing searing neck pains. "It's crazy as hell." Even Moody, who never ate anything unhealthy or neglected going to the gym, started losing his mind. For a few days he thought he'd lost his keys, or had them stolen. He sent out an e-mail and eventually posted a flyer offering a reward for their return. He asked *everyone* if he or she had seen his keys. But it turned out they were where he'd left them—in his briefcase. A few weeks later, Moody would get in trouble for shoving a security guard in the chest.

The challenge was a three-headed monster, according to Cubias. "First, there are the numbers. There are just too many kids. Next, there's the fact that we don't have your average Green Dot kids; these kids are further behind. Then there are the people we inherited, the clerks and office workers. We have to deal with all three of these things every day."

Teachers and administrators were slap-happy by 3:00, unable to do much more than watch after-school sports to unwind. They talked about falling asleep as soon as they got home, or staying up until two or three in the morning working on a presentation or a lesson. There was no time to do laundry or go to the ATM, much less make it to a doctor's appointment. Then they got up and did it all again the next morning. Talking to them was like talking to someone during finals; after about ten seconds, you'd lose them to some other thought. It wasn't clear that they were taking in what was being said to them. They couldn't stay still for long. Something usually interrupted them—a student, a teacher, a parent, or the crackling radio.

Problems with student behavior were a small but persistent issue that, despite the much-improved orderliness on campus, never really disappeared. Coleman's string of days without a fight was cut short at three. The boys' bathroom just off the quad was the scene of a couple of lunchtime fights that were videotaped and put up on YouTube. Then, a few weeks later, a couple of kids snuck onto the third-story roof of the main building and tossed a fire extinguisher into the parking lot, hitting the hood of a new teacher's car.

Keeping students in uniform all the time turned out to be a crushingly repetitive task for Cubias and others. Most kids complied fairly easily, but a large number came up with a hundred excuses. *My uniform was dirty. I wore something black. I couldn't find it. It's too hot. The [uniform] loan room was closed. I hate that thing.* At one point, an exhausted Cubias started using a toy megaphone to remind kids to stay in uniform while on campus. Bought at a discount store for $10, the blue-and-white plastic device had a memory chip that allowed Cubias to record any message and repeat it with the simple push of a button: "Please make sure your shirts are tucked in," blared the recorded message. "Please tuck in your shirts. Thank you." The kids hated it. Cubias couldn't get enough. During lunchtime and break periods, he would walk up to students with untucked shirts and hit the button on the megaphone. If necessary, he would move the megaphone up next to a student's ear. Sometimes he would just stand in the middle of the hallway and hold the megaphone above his head, sipping coffee out of his coffee mug and pressing the button as many times as needed.

Despite all their creativity, teachers and staff were so busy taking care of moment-to-moment tasks like supervision and student discipline that they couldn't take care of chronic issues like fixing the curriculum skills class, coming up with a system to track detention time, or figuring out which teachers were floundering worse than others. Professional development sessions were planned and pulled together in a rush at the last minute. Meetings were constantly being rescheduled, delaying decisions. Teachers and administrators were in a fog. As October turned into November, it was clear that the pace was breaking them down.

"You guys are really empty on shout-outs today," said Coleman at one of the weekly faculty meetings.

To some extent, the disorganization and overcrowding were offset by the excitement of being part of something new and uncertain, part of a group of people pulling toward a common, perhaps unattainable goal. At times working at Locke could be heady. Cameron Diaz had been on campus. Bill Gates came by for a tour. Lisa Ling and her camera crew were following teachers and administrators around—not to mention local print, TV, and radio reporters. All eyes were on Locke, it seemed. It was like working for a start-up company on the verge of going public, or finishing a dissertation. It was the hardest thing they'd ever done.

The teachers weren't the only ones working hard but lacking experience. Green Dot had never served students with severe disabilities, or more than a handful of kids returning from juvenile detention (also known as "camp"), or large numbers of kids who were so far behind on their credits. It had never tried to fix a full-size neighborhood high school, and was relying on its old small-school model rather than starting from scratch or studying other turnarounds. ("There just wasn't time to do all that," said then Green Dot COO Petruzzi.) But the staffing and budgets from the old model didn't really fit. Administrators at Locke needed timely guidance on discipline, attendance, testing, and evaluation procedures. Locke kids needed enhanced support services and remedial literacy help. Perhaps the most obvious problem was that kids were dropping out in droves from Locke 4, the alternative school tucked into the middle of the campus, or showing up but not making much progress toward graduation. Green Dot was trying to avoid the perception that it was turning into "another LAUSD"—a slow, expensive, and inflexible organization rather than one that was as accountable to schools as it asked schools to be to students—but found itself similarly boxed in by budgetary, human capital, and logistical concerns.

"Holy shit, this is harder than we thought," said Petruzzi.

Sometimes, the way Green Dot treated Locke was infuriating in the extreme. One day Cubias found one of the IT guys from the Green Dot office in the equipment room at Locke loading LCD projectors onto a cart, destination unknown. LCD projectors have become a key piece of classroom equipment these days—the modern equivalent of the overhead projector—and Cubias guarded Locke's resources jealously. The technician wouldn't let Cubias see the full list of where the equipment was supposed to go; Cubias refused to let him take any more projectors. They stood there, stalemated, until Coleman helped sort out what was going on.

"I feel that 'I told you so' mentality settling in," said Cubias after yet another useless meeting with Green Dot administrators at which his impassioned complaints went nowhere. His increasingly plaintive warnings weren't being heeded. Maybe handing

Locke over to Green Dot had been an unwise move. Frustrated as he was, however, Cubias never lost his impish sense of humor. For Halloween that year, he came as himself—Zeus—complete with robe, beard, and cardboard thunderbolt.

By and large, Coleman took the opposite approach, keeping her cool in meetings and trying to keep everyone happy. She knew that there was serious grumbling among her staff. She agreed with Cubias and others that Big Locke was getting particularly shortchanged. Yet she didn't push Green Dot on behalf of her teachers and students; she never really went "all mama bear" on them, as she liked to put it. The only time anyone saw Coleman really blow up that fall was the time she saw the camera crew from *Nightline* delaying the start of class while they finished up an interview with a teacher. "We felt like we were teenagers in the principal's office," said Green Dot press person Tracy Mallozzi. Most of the time, Coleman just hunkered down and did the job put in front of her as best she could.

In the end, Locke's most persistent advocate for the school would be neither an administrator nor a longtime Locke teacher but rather the mild-mannered drama teacher, Monica Mayall, who had arrived at the school only a few weeks before.

11

MAYALL'S REVENGE

Drama and art teacher Monica Mayall stood in the doorway checking students into her bright, spacious third-floor classroom. Most got a warm welcome. New faces not already on her roster received a polite rebuff, however.

"Sorry, you're number 34, so I can't let you in," said Mayall with a cheerful smile. "It's nothing personal—I hope to have you back in my class someday."

The students, many with a newly printed schedule in their hands, looked surprised but headed back downstairs to the counselors' office.

"But you don't have thirty-three kids your room," said Kaplowitz, the counselor who came up to Mayall's classroom to see what the problem was after several students said they'd been kicked out of art. Indeed, on any given day the twice-divorced mother of two college-age boys had nowhere near thirty-three kids in her room. But that wasn't the point. "The contract says I only have to take thirty-three on my roster," said Mayall, who often had a sneaky little smile on her face. "Take some of the kids who aren't showing up off my roster and then I'll have room."

Like every other teacher at Locke, Mayall was only required to take 33 kids in her class, but she and many others were being asked to take in many more than that—35, 40, even 45 students at a time. Mayall—one of the most experienced classroom teachers on campus—was making counselors and administrators stick to the class-size targets that were part of Green Dot's core "tenets" and part of the contract that governed teachers' workloads.

For several weeks, she went through the same drill, refusing to take any more students and befuddling the overworked counselors. "Yeah, sorry, I'm going to keep doing that," Mayall would tell them.

Mayall didn't look like a rabble-rouser. She had pretty green eyes and a high, tiny voice she described as a Minnie Mouse squeak. She wore high-waisted "mom" jeans and comfortable patterned tops and gym shoes and constantly pushed her dirty blonde hair back behind her ear. She hadn't meant to be a teacher, but thought it would be a good career for a single mom and then found out she liked it. She had started out extremely excited about the Green Dot model, applying online from Seattle and then flying down to do interviews, visit the school, and meet Coleman in person. She wanting to make sure she wasn't going to end up working for another tyrannical principal, like the one she'd had in the Seattle public school system. Coleman passed the test, and seemed to want Mayall for her ideas about what she could do with drama and her enthusiasm for the turnaround effort. (It didn't hurt that Mayall was certified to teach English, art, and social studies and was willing to teach summer school.)

Mayall knew that administrators—charter or district— oftentimes played a part in chewing up and spitting out teachers with paperwork and work demands. In fact, some charter schools were known to be especially hard on teachers. But she was still hopeful and idealistic enough to come to Locke. After her interview with Coleman, she had been invited to a Friday happy hour on the roof at the Green Dot home office, where they played with light sabers. She was hooked. "I *so* wanted to work with these people," she said. "They seemed very cool."

Since starting at Locke, however, Mayall had fallen into a serious funk. The first red flag was the overcrowding situation that had caught Mayall's eye over the summer. Months before school was set to start, Green Dot had already signed up twelve hundred Locke students to attend Big Locke, which would mean six hundred students for the black side and six hundred for the white side. More students would likely show up in September. She warned Cubias and Coleman and was dismayed to learn that Green Dot had initially planned for there to be three schools within Big Locke but had rolled those plans back, unsure about enrollment numbers. However many older kids showed up, there would be just two schools to handle them. The second issue was the burned-out theater space she'd hoped to use. Coleman had showed Mayall the little theater located just off the quad during her on-campus interview and told the award-winning drama teacher she could have it if she took the job. The walls were black from smoke and covered with graffiti, but it had a stage and a raked floor with bolts where the seats had once been attached. Mayall reached out to her far-flung contacts and secured pledges of lights and curtains and other supplies, only to find out a few weeks later that donations had to be approved by the district, which still owned the facility. It soon became clear: the theater wasn't going to get renovated anytime soon. Demoralized and embarrassed, Mayall had to tell her colleagues that she'd spoken too soon. It was all her bad experiences with school districts all over again.

From Green Dot's side of things, uncertainties about hiring Mayall started popping up almost immediately, too. She had two school-issued laptops stolen from her room over the summer. She asked for (and got) a schedule without early-morning classes and began doing her class preparation at home to avoid being asked to cover classes for others. She wasn't particularly strong at classroom management, so kids came and left her airy, bright third-floor classroom and frequently ignored her instructions (as they did with several other teachers). She took days off as often as she felt she needed to, always careful to make sure her colleagues and supervisors knew ahead of time. (Her absences, not coincidentally, tended to be on days when Green Dot had planned professional development.) As head of the art and drama department, Mayall's first decision was to cancel all future departmental meetings "until I get in trouble with Ronnie." She told her colleagues—all of them much younger and less experienced than she—how to avoid getting cornered into covering classes during their prep periods and to take care of themselves first. " 'Oh, but it's for the kids,' is how they will approach you," Mayall said. "But you have the option of saying 'no.' Someone else's lack of planning does not create an emergency for you."

Who could blame her? Administrative meetings were the bane of most teachers' existence. Rookie teachers were easy marks for administrators needing a simple alternative to calling in a substitute; Cubias and Boulden prowled the hallways every morning looking for available teachers to avoid having to bring in a substitute. Mayall had seen it all in her previous schools. She was a one-woman lesson in how veteran teachers think and behave, conserving energy and effort, always defending against misguided administrative decrees. From Green Dot's perspective, she was a potential "culture killer," a negative, disruptive voice that hindered the teamwork and flexibility needed to make the turnaround work.

It was as an advocate for other teachers that Mayall would cause administrators the most difficulty. The biggest problem Locke was facing was one of too many kids and not enough teachers. As Mayall and others had anticipated, Green Dot had underestimated the number of kids who were going to show up to school and was slow to respond to the influx. As a charter organization, Green Dot was used to having control over enrollment. Each school Green Dot had started in the past was allowed to enroll a certain amount of kids, and that was it. But this wasn't the situation here. Any school-age child who lived in the neighborhood was allowed to go to Locke, no matter when during the year. And now, as word was spreading that the new Locke might be worth a try, parents were signing their children up to attend the school two, three, four weeks into the school year. More kids were showing up every day. There were simply too many kids signing up to go to the school, and no way to stop the flow.

"I don't know where to put kids," said an exasperated Coleman. "I've got brand-new teachers with thirty-five and forty kids. Who's letting these kids in?"

Green Dot had promised significant resources to decrease class size, personalized instruction, and extensive academic interventions—but little of that was happening. Coleman didn't have enough teachers, and the district said that Locke wasn't technically full (a complex calculation based on square footage and other factors). There were lots of unused rooms on campus, and Green Dot had committed to serve everyone. First, newly arrived kids were sent to Hobbs Hall, the multipurpose room located next to the covered lunch area. Once their paperwork was processed, they would be given a schedule and sent to class. But guidance counselors like Kaplowitz were quickly running out of room, so some students were being sent to the library, which remained only partially repaired from the previous year's fire. Some of them would end up there the entire first semester of school—all the way to February—taught by a substitute. Veteran teachers like English teacher Maggie Bushek were furious that Locke kids were being stuffed into classrooms or given schedules that didn't help them. "Our kids have put up with the most bullshit and deserve to get the most out of this transformation," said Bushek with typical bluntness.

Watching Cubias, Coleman, and the classroom teachers deal with the oversized school was extremely unpleasant. They were helpless; they were mad—when they had time to think about what was being done to them. And the answers they were getting from the home office didn't really make sense. Green Dot's failure to follow through on the promised theater space, plus the inexperience and obliviousness she saw from Green Dot's response to the overcrowding issue, stoked Mayall's desire to hold the organization's feet to the fire. She had an intense dislike for injustice and unmet promises.

"I had an axe to grind," she admitted. "If they'd given me my little theater and let me do my thing, I would have probably minded my own business."

What did Mayall do? She became the union representative for Big Locke and began communicating teachers' concerns and complaints about class size and other workload issues to the union president and Locke senior management. Campus aides weren't in the halls when they were needed. Classroom phones didn't work. The bells rang at random moments—worse than having no bells at all. Counselors and administrators sent notes to students during the middle of class, another bothersome interruption. "She grieved a litany of things," said Coleman. "Some things I had bullheadedly gone into, trampling toes. Other things I was like, 'Come on, Monica. How ticky-tacky are you going to get?'"

But class size wasn't a small issue, and wasn't just a matter of teachers' workloads. Green Dot was receiving federal class-size reduction funds, which ostensibly brought class sizes down to twenty-eight for certain core academic subjects. The school could lose funding if the class sizes weren't reduced. For weeks, Mayall bugged everyone who would listen to her about the class sizes being too big. She talked about the issue at faculty meetings. She talked to Coleman. She talked to Green Dot people when they came on campus. Then, in mid-October, Mayall and the union filed a grievance against Green Dot over the class-size issue—the first such grievance filed in the organization's history. There were thirty-six classes with over thirty-three students.

Officially, Green Dot welcomed concerns from teachers. But in practice, dealing with teachers' complaints was complicated, and taking action could be expensive. Green Dot wanted to make sure that teachers' class loads were "balanced"—spread so that class sizes were even from section to section—before hiring anyone else. And it had the law on its side. Although the Green Dot talking points were clear about class size, the actual contract language merely set a *target* of twenty-four kids per class, and required conversations and unspecified relief measures. There was no hard-and-fast requirement that Green Dot hire more teachers or pay its current ones more as compensation (as is done in many districts). This was no matter to Mayall; she would bother and embarrass administrators into responding even if they didn't legally have to. She was pesky and persistent—annoyingly polite and impervious to the glances and hints that she should be a team player along with everyone else. She wasn't giving up, either, sweet and relentless, annoying even those who agreed with her. Then in early November her case was bolstered when a rookie teacher was attacked by a special education student in one of the overstuffed classrooms. "I did not sign up for this," wrote the teacher in a desperate e-mail, noting that there were several special education students in the classroom but none of the classroom aides that were supposed to be there to help. "PLEASE COME TO MY CLASS." He didn't come back the next day, and quit shortly thereafter.

Contract or no, it seemed clear after this incident that if something didn't happen, other teachers would start leaving—at the end of the year if not before. Green Dot claimed a 90 percent retention rate for its teachers in the past. But a mass exodus from Locke could lower that number quickly. Pushing her case even harder, Mayall sent a strongly worded letter to Coleman, the senior managers at Green Dot, and the union: "Our students are not getting the intervention or support they need to master the curriculum—due in part to the sheer size of our school and the need for more instructors and smaller class sizes," she wrote. "This is a disservice to these students as well as a disruption to the classes already in progress which they are entering."

The letter hit Coleman hard. She came to Mayall's classroom after school and—briefly—broke down, blinking through tears and valiantly trying to stop her lip from trembling. She was new at the job. She was doing her best. She couldn't control the district or Green Dot. It was an impossible situation. "She was exhausted and overwhelmed, trying to do everything she could manage," said Mayall, who didn't actually blame Coleman. "Green Dot didn't really have any idea of what they were getting into." After the fact, Coleman was glad Mayall had taken action. "I'm more desperate for the help than I'm worried about the union thing," she said. Cubias felt the same way, encouraging Mayall to press Green Dot into taking action. He'd been promised a small school of about five hundred kids, but was instead dealing with a school of more than eight hundred.

In the end, there was no dramatic response from Green Dot, no sudden hiring spree or ban on oversized classes. The union met with Green Dot to talk about teachers who were over the limit; administrators met with the affected teachers and, eventually, made a handful of additional hires. Teachers with the impacted classrooms "agreed" to retain more than thirty-three students per class. Seniors with enough credits were pulled out of classes and scheduled into "service" positions in various offices around the school, filing papers or answering phones. But these changes were enough. As of February, just two teachers had resigned—far fewer than in previous years—and over 80 percent of teachers would sign up to return for a second year, compared to the past standard of about 50 percent. Even those who weren't directly affected—or who were deeply suspicious of teachers unions from past experiences—were glad to know that Mayall was voicing their concerns up the chain of command. "At least the teacher's side was being aired," said English teacher Sully.

Whether or not teachers at Locke paid much attention, Green Dot took the contract seriously, creating an invisible safety net under the hard work being done in the classroom. The contract didn't intrude on school life very much, day to day, but when needed it was there, and proved to be sturdy both during the first year of the Locke turnaround as well as during future years, when growth and consolidation would create an even greater need for established structures.

12

ROGUE COPS

On a sunny Friday afternoon in January, about an hour after school let out, a group of students started shooting dice. They were gathered in the cafeteria, which at Locke High School was a deep, covered space right off the sunny quad, with blue-painted metal lunch tables fixed in rows. In the quad, drill team members spun their flags in the air, and Junior ROTC kids marched around in endless circles. Sun shone into the front side of the cafeteria, but the teens inside were shaded.

The group—maybe fifteen of them—stood in a loose half-circle. Most of them were athletes, many of them on the football team: Kenny. Darnell. David. Anthony. Kerón. All black kids, all boys. They were older—most of them juniors or seniors—nearly all of them black shirts under Cubias's supervision. Still in uniform for the most part, they were just passing the time, waiting for the basketball game to start. They weren't making much effort to conceal themselves.

"Can anybody spread this thing out?" said Darnell, a greyhound-thin senior. "I need to make some money."

Making money was a big part of life for Locke students, many of whom didn't get allowances from parents or have access to regular teenage jobs. There weren't many chain stores or malls in the neighborhood. There weren't even that many fast-food joints. So some Locke kids sold junk food in the halls during the morning break. Others designed flyers for parties. A few sold pot. And some played dice before and after (and sometimes during) school. Green Dot had done its best to eradicate the practice—confiscating dice and patrolling as much of the campus as possible, but the gambling wasn't entirely gone. You could still occasionally find kids huddled around a pair of red dice in unused corners of the massive campus.

The dice games weren't usually this large or this public, however. Yet for almost an hour no one seemed to notice or care what was going on. A few kids sitting at the nearby cafeteria lunch tables pored over fantasy game cards they collected and traded out of big three-ring binders. A pair of security guards zoomed by on their beloved golf cart, but they either didn't look over or couldn't see into the shadows. There should have been a guard posted on the quad to look out for just this kind of thing, but none appeared. Then, just before 5:00 P.M., tipped off by a Junior ROTC instructor who happened to glance over and see what was happening, a half-dozen security guards rushed around the corner and flooded into the cafeteria.

"Don't anybody move," yelled Lieutenant Alex Moore, striding toward the group at a fast walk. "Don't *anybody* move."

Nearly as wide as he was tall, Moore was in charge of keeping the school and the surrounding streets safe for Locke kids. As he walked toward the dice-playing kids, his voice was loud and deep, and he was shaking a can of pepper spray up and down. The metal ball inside the grey canister clacked back and forth. The can sounded full.

The use of pepper spray on students had a long, sad history at Locke. Guards liked it because it was effective but nonlethal. Kids feared it because of the stinging, gagging effect it had on their eyes and mouths. "Hell, we used to spray kids every day," said one guard. Having such a large squad of private security guards on campus was something new, however. Where previous school administrations had relied on a handful of unarmed campus aides, two school police officers, and one or two private guards, Green Dot had nine guards to protect the school, along with a couple of particularly tough-looking dudes who were hired to stand outside the school at dismissal time each day—so-called gang interventionists. To those concerned about last year's violence, including parents who frequently asked about security measures, these were necessary steps. To those unfazed—or numb—the guards and guns were overkill.

Of course, the dice-playing boys scattered instead of doing as they were told, laughing and calling out to each other as they ran in different directions. This was the easiest game of tag ever, teenage athletes running away from adult guards weighed down by guns and flashlights—especially considering that the guards forgot to block the open cafeteria exits. Some kids didn't even bother running all that far—a few quick steps and they stopped and turned, looking to see if anyone was going to chase them. One student didn't run, however. He stood there, still, towering above Moore and the other couple of officers gathered around him. His name was Kerón, a seventeen-year-old junior with a boyish face but the body of a full-grown man. He was the defensive star of the Locke football team and was already being recruited by the University of Southern California. He wore his hair cropped close to his head, making his ears stand out on the sides. Football wasn't Kerón's only talent. Kids and teachers alike told stories about his one-punch knockout power. "He's a beast," said Cubias. "He'll fuck you up." Indeed, Kerón had already been in a couple of fights on campus this year, and had been arrested and cited in the past—including during the campus-wide melee that shut down the school and brought national media attention the year before. Yet Kerón was also extremely polite and respectful around most adults—an unusual trait that Cubias admired. Others thought it was an act.

Green Dot had turned to a local guy, a former Locke security guard, to find and train the expanded security team. Called CRST (Conflict Resolution Suppression Team), the newly created company had a handful of other schools under contract along with Locke. The guards wore dark-green polo shirts or windbreakers, tan tactical pants with reinforced knees, and ankle-high boots. A couple wore sunglasses and black gloves along with belts that held handcuffs, ammunition clips, and pepper spray. They patrolled the neighborhood before and after school and backed up teachers and administrators who were having any trouble with students in the classrooms and halls. Their leader, Moore, known to most as "LT," spent most of the time in his office supervising other guards or in his patrol car rather than interacting with kids in "the towers," as he liked to call the main school building. Strict and earnest around the kids, Moore was gentle and laughed easily off duty.

Kerón stood there looking around, waiting to see what Moore and his men would try next. His arms were at his sides, his mouth slightly open, giving him a quizzical expression. Moore told the boy to sit at a nearby table, but Kerón didn't react fast enough. Fearing an escape or a fight, Moore reached behind his back with his left hand and pulled out a pair of handcuffs to try to restrain the student. But the much larger boy didn't much want to be handcuffed, and shrugged his arm away, throwing Moore off balance. The lieutenant gathered himself, stepped back, raised his right hand, and pushed the button on top of the pepper spray canister. A thick stream of liquid blasted straight toward Kerón's face.

••

This was exactly the situation that some Locke veterans most feared—an unnecessary opportunity for conflicts with students. "It's like a police state over there," said former Locke teacher Reggie Andrews, who came on campus once in a while to check on former students. The kids mocked the guards for their lowly status as "rent-a-cops." Someone on the Locke staff described them as "minimally trained guys with guns." The guards didn't generally hold any malice toward the kids, but they didn't have any illusions about them, either. They saw the kids out on the streets, at their defiant worst, while teachers usually saw them only at their best. Mostly accustomed to working at malls and housing projects and strip clubs, the guards hadn't been trained in how to deal with kids on a school campus. Some adults worried about whether having all these untrained guys with guns on campus was a good idea. "They're good enough for the students we got now," said Coach Crawford, a longtime dean at the school. "But it would've been real bad if we had the kids we had last year, though. Somebody would've got a gun off of them. Somebody would've got shot."

The guards were there because Green Dot was determined that there wouldn't be a repeat of last year's chaos, that the campus would be safe and orderly, and that the hectic streets outside wouldn't be able to find their way inside the school. Like an international nation-building effort, first came safety and security—"hard power," if you will. And it was working, by and large. The campus felt strangely—deceptively—safe. (It was the safest place in all of South Central, joked some of the teachers.)

There was very little tagging, ditching, smoking, or fighting. When needed, the guards helped teachers get kids settled and heading toward Moody's office, where Moody would talk them down, figure out the problem, and assign detention or make a call home.

"Kids mouth off to us, and we don't take personally," said one of the guards. "We stay professional, and take them to the dean, who backs us up."

The need for extra security had been pretty clear at the start of the year. "Every day the first few weeks there was Bounty Hunters and SouthLos coming around here to start something," said one of the guards. "They were looking for rivals, or someone to get into it, or for new members." Then a bunch of suspected gangbangers came onto campus after school, claiming to have a relative playing in a basketball game. The security guards arrived at the gym en masse and kindly asked them to leave. The dangers and momentary conflicts hadn't gone away entirely since then, either. Young tattooed men with nicknames like Sniper sometimes came to the front gate, asking to come inside or to know whether a particular student was there. By the end of the second year, the guards would have collected a bucketful of knives, prison-style shanks, and realistic looking toy guns.

Not everyone was against having them around. Kaplowitz, for one, preferred having them on campus than not. Bumbling as they sometimes could be, they were an effective deterrent and useful in breaking up fights between larger kids. Barr thought the armed guards were a clear necessity, given past incidents at other Green Dot schools. And even with all the guards posted around the school, Locke had little of the confined, dark feel of other urban schools. The hallways were wide. The ceilings were tall. There were no metal detectors to go through, or drug-sniffing dogs, or ID checks. Almost everywhere on campus, there was lots of room to spread out, and abundant light.

"All this good stuff around here wouldn't happen without CRST," said one of the guards.

••

Kerón saw the stream of liquid coming toward him, but didn't have time to get out of the way. It hit him on the right side of his face and went straight into his eye. He squinted his face and put his hand up to his eye, but he wasn't immobilized and seemed not to hear Moore's shouted commands to stop and let himself be handcuffed. Instead, Kerón walked out of the cafeteria, past the leafy quad, and out onto Saint Street. Following behind, Moore radioed his men to lock the front gates and called for backup. Kerón wasn't sure where he was going. His eye hurt. He pushed his hand against his eyeball, trying to squeeze the pain away. He didn't want to fight. He was trying to stay calm.

The next person Kerón ran into was Vic Lopez, coach of the JV football team and one of the campus aides. A thirty-seven-year-old father of two who wore his hair in a tight ponytail and nearly always had a book in hand to help pass the time, Lopez was working the front door of the basketball game, taking money for tickets to get into the gym. Seeing Kerón walk by with the guards close behind him, he called out and told the boy to come over. But Lopez wasn't trying to get Kerón to go along with Moore. Lopez hated the new security guards as much as he hated the kids who tried to get away with scrawling graffiti in the halls he patrolled. Both were affronts to his keenly developed sense of order. Lopez moved Kerón behind him against the side of the gymnasium and turned toward Moore and his men.

"You guys need to hold off," said Lopez. His voice was flat, his face expressionless. His feet were planted wide, his hands pushed deep into the pockets of his pants. Behind him, Kerón rubbed his eyes. Lopez looked down at the handcuffs Moore still had in his small hands and shook his head. "That ain't gonna happen." The message was clear: Moore would need to go through Lopez if he wanted to get to Kerón. Later on he would say that he was trying to protect the guards as much as he was protecting Kerón. The guards stood there, looking at each other. Moore wasn't sure what to do. Students and parents walked by, entering and leaving the gymnasium, where the JV basketball game was ending and the varsity game would soon start. It was a standoff.

Back in the main building, Cubias was packing up his office when he saw a couple of kids and guards running down the hallway outside his office. It was a Friday. It was the first week back after Christmas vacation, and Cubias and the rest of the Locke staff had used most of their time off to get some much-needed rest and try to figure out a way to make it through to the end of the year. He was hoping to go home at a decent hour, but then he got on the radio and started asking what was happening. He started walking toward the gymnasium, leaning forward as he went. He had a black walkie-talkie in one hand, his massive keychain and long blue lanyard in the other. He was furious.

Once Cubias arrived at the gym, his first concern was getting the spray washed out of Kerón's eyes. Locke kids who'd been sprayed compared the sensation to being blinded or poked in the eye. They would have to pry their eyelids open with their fingers to wash the chemical out. "You can't open your eyes no matter how hard you try," said a student who'd been sprayed in the past. The taste in your mouth—foul and gagging—was reportedly even worse. Cubias and Crawford and a couple of other guards took Kerón to the bathroom, and then they all headed to the security bungalow, a double-wide trailer located just off the quad. Kerón sat quietly on one of the chairs, hunched over and silent. He was wearing a white undershirt and khaki pants, and held his black uniform shirt in one hand. Moore gave his version of what had happened, a story that now included an attempted assault on the part of Kerón for which he'd already called the school police. "I asked him several times to stop, then told him to move over toward the table," said Moore. "He said 'I ain't going nowhere' and 'You can't touch me.' Then he bucked up against me. So I stepped back and sprayed him. I was protecting myself." Some of the other officers backed Moore up, saying that Kerón had balled his fist and was about to lash out. Kerón didn't say anything, though he would later say that Moore was grabbing at him and yelling. "I told him to stop grabbing at me," said Kerón. "He ain't my father."

Cubias wasn't buying any of what Moore was saying—not even the parts about the massive dice game and disobedient kids that were accurate. He was furious that no one on the security team was supervising the quad after school and that the security team had rushed at the dice players so ill-advisedly. And he sensed that Moore was just embarrassed that he'd gotten shown up. That the incident had resulted in a Locke student's getting pepper-sprayed—and accused of raising his fist against Moore—was too much for Cubias to stand.

"I'm not OK with this—I'm not cool with pepper-spraying kids," said Cubias, his voice high and scratchy. "You don't call the police—I do. There were four administrators on campus, but we weren't informed." A few minutes later, Cubias was pacing outside the security bungalow on the phone with Moore's boss, Eddie Goodman, who was trying to defend Moore's actions.

"I'm not going to sit around and have your officers run around like a bunch of rogue cops," said Cubias. "They shouldn't be doing things that they don't have the training or the intelligence to do." He was desperate to avoid having Locke go back to being a place where interactions between adults and students got physical. He and other school staff were trying to implement their own school safety program—a more diplomatic approach given the fancy name of "positive behavior intervention." Friendly but firm, staff addressed students in extremely polite terms, calling students over individually rather than speaking to them from afar or in groups. There was a lot of praise given out, and every effort was made to avoid direct physical confrontations. Even chasing kids was something they tried not to do. This was the "soft power" side to Green Dot's turnaround effort—the part that focused on winning hearts and minds rather than enforcing compliance. This pepper-spraying incident was actually the second in a month. Yet even in the heat of the moment, Cubias's calling the guards "rogue cops" and questioning their intelligence was a low blow. Cubias knew that the guards had good intentions, trying their hardest to do a difficult, occasionally frightening job. He knew they hadn't been trained or supervised properly. He knew that they were all that stood between Locke and the surrounding community, and had done a lot of good in the first few weeks of the year. "I was just really, really, fucking furious," said Cubias afterwards.

Back outside the security bungalow, the sun had gone down. Orange lights illuminated the steps in front of the security bungalow, but the rest of the quad was dark. A full moon rose above the campus. Officers Terry and Palacio showed up, the same ones who had been at the melee the year before, and everyone told his story to the officers again. (The guards could stop kids, search them, and tell them to stay away from the school, but they couldn't arrest anyone.) The police officers wrote out a citation and gave Kerón a March court date. Still sitting on a chair in the security bungalow, Kerón called his mom—a security guard at another school—and explained what had happened. "Yeah, just like last time," he said in a soft voice.

This time, Cubias was able to protect Kerón. He had to apologize for his tirade the next day, but he helped get the ticket against Kerón dismissed and made clear that the boy wasn't to be targeted, despite his size and reputation. Eventually, Cubias and the guards would work out a protocol that governed what the security team did when dealing with kids on campus—most of the time it involved calling an administrator and keeping the police out of it. There were weekly meetings. The differences in worldviews never really went away, but the communication and understanding got much better. The teachers realized that the guards weren't out to hurt the kids, and the guards came to understand how circumscribed the teachers' views of the kids could be and where they fit in.

13

"MAY"-HEM

One sunny morning just before the start of school, dean of students Mike Moody stood outside the gate urging kids to hustle into the building before the bell rang.

"Get inside, people, the bell's about to ring," he yelled out to black-shirted students walking slowly across 111th Street.

Wraparound sunglasses on his bald head and a black walkie-talkie in hand, the former Division I college football player was serious about getting kids to class on time and pretty much everything else. His jeans were pressed, and his gym shoes were bright white. It was a rare sight to see him dressed so casually. Cubias's right-hand man on the black side, Moody was fair but firm. If you didn't make it in time, you had to wait. If you messed up worse than that, Moody would give you detention or—even worse—a lengthy talking to.

It was the first week of May, the beginning of the long eight-week slog from now through to Locke's late-June graduation. May also brought the beginning of the annual testing season—the tiresome monthlong process that would produce the rating used by many to gauge Locke's success. Graffiti was starting to pop up more often. Once again, kids were sneaking into unused rooms to smoke and play dice.

Most students passed Moody and headed to class, hoping to make it before the doors locked. Then, just a few minutes before the 8:00 o'clock bell, a senior named David sauntered through the gate and onto school grounds. Small and dark-skinned, David had big, deep-set eyes and a wide, expressive mouth. He wore an oversized baseball cap whose edge extended out past his ears and carried a skateboard in one hand. The outfit made him look smaller and younger than he was—like a little kid headed to the skate park rather than a senior heading toward graduation. A few seconds later, David came out of the gate, standing a few feet in front of Moody on the sidewalk in front of the school.

"Go inside, David," said Moody. "You don't want to be late."

But David didn't move. He wanted to hang out on the sidewalk until the very last minute before the gate was closed, enjoying every last moment of freedom and perhaps hoping to get under Moody's skin a bit. He slowly looked up and down 111th Street for any sign of his friends. A couple more times, Moody told David to go inside. The boy glanced back but didn't say anything. Finally, Moody told the teen that he would be barred from campus for the day if he didn't go inside immediately.

"Either you want to be here or you don't," said Moody. "I'm not putting up with any more of this stuff."

David smiled but didn't move fast enough. Moody waved to the security guard to step inside the gate; he closed and locked the gate with a chain and a big silver padlock. Then he radioed the other gates not to let David into the school, and went to get ready to deal with the tardy line. David stood there looking surprised, a thin smile fixed on his face.

The challenge of these last two long months of school wasn't just holding down vandalism and fighting. All over campus, Locke students were struggling to keep their grades up, teachers were struggling to keep things focused in the classroom, and administrators were trying to keep up with events and decisions coming at them fast and furious. Kids who had somehow held it together all year were now in danger of failing classes and not graduating if they didn't stay or get back on track. The school was a lot more crowded than usual at this time of the year. And there were lots of social distractions. Senior prom, scheduled for the end of the week, was everyone's most immediate focus. Students and administrators wanted the first prom for the new Locke to be a hit. Most of all, Cubias and Coleman and everyone else who'd put in countless hours over the past year didn't want to lose all the ground they felt they'd gained.

Standing outside the gate, David texted his counselor, Miss Kaplowitz, to let her know what had happened. She'd called and woken him up for school that morning, and stopped by to pick him up on the way. What David didn't know was that, just the day before, Moody had sent an e-mail to his colleagues describing David's long record of infractions and unmet promises to improve, making the case that David had used up all his chances and needed to go—to be "finalized," in Locke terminology, or even sent to another school—rather than stay and have a chance at graduating with the rest of his class. He'd been caught red-eyed and high during school, and had been accused of selling pot to other kids but never caught in the act. The boy didn't even live in Locke's attendance area anymore; technically he wasn't even supposed to be going to this school. This morning's bit of silliness with Moody at the front gate only confirmed it. David was handsome, disrespectful, manipulative, smart—intensely frustrating to work with. After dealing with him since summer school—almost nine months—Moody had had enough.

David had the ease and confidence of the athlete he was, and sometimes let out with an amusing comment (often at someone else's expense). The younger boys seemed to look up to him, but he often stood alone during lunch. He spent most of his time with his girlfriend, a senior on the white side. He didn't show the respect that teachers and administrators expected (or the fear that they sometimes seemed to want). "He's one of those guys who, if you tell him not to slam the door, he'll stand there and smile at you and slam the door," said Stephen Minix, the head of the athletic department at Locke. "Most guys who are doing bad things avoid me," said Coach Vic. "David walked up and introduced himself. He asked me for a ride home." Perhaps most frustrating of all, David wasn't coming anywhere close to living up to his academic potential. A sharp mind, he had taken to failing his classes and then making up a slew of assignments at the last minute.

Putting kids out of school wasn't something that hadn't already been done that year. Moody and Cubias had already kicked out a handful of kids, or transferred them to other parts of the Locke cluster. Moody kept detailed records about referrals and incidents, and most cases were pretty easy to decide, but it was still the first year of the new Locke, and there wasn't any clear-cut system for deciding these discipline cases. Exhausted administrators were making decisions on a case-by-case, somewhat haphazard basis. Sometimes they went through the formal process called a DRB (Disciplinary Review Board). Others times students were given help finding another place—a decision that few students or parents knew they could challenge.

Ten minutes after the morning bell rang, Moody was sitting at the folding table set up just outside the front doors to the main building, looking down at his laptop and checking off the names of tardy students as they arrived. Every day there were about a hundred students on the black side who showed up a few minutes late and had to be checked in and given detention time for their crime. The door to the main building opened from the inside, and counselor Emily Kaplowitz emerged. Keys and cell phone in hand, she came up and stood there in the sunlight right next to Moody.

"What's the problem, Mike?" she asked.

Dark-haired with short lacquered nails, Kaplowitz was known to most as "Miss K." Curvy and stylish, she nearly always carried her cell phone and file folders in her arms in front of her. She lived in Hollywood with her film school boyfriend and a little dog named Winston.

"The answer is no," said Moody, not looking up from his computer spreadsheet.

Kaplowitz just stood there, expressionless, waiting. Behind Kaplowitz's usual smile was a determined, fiercely competitive personality. She charmed the boys and befriended the girls. Sweetly but persistently, she badgered teachers to give students extra chances and makeup work.

Moody entered a couple more kids' names.

"Miss K, the answer is no," repeated Moody, still looking down. "He's going to be expelled. He's failing every class."

Again, Kaplowitz said nothing. She just stood there looking at the back of Moody's head.

"Good morning to you," said Moody, pecking away at his computer.

Finally, she turned and headed back inside, then stopped and turned again. "He's going to miss a whole day of school just because he's late," she spat out. Then she was gone.

••

Considering everything else going on at Locke, guidance counselors like Kaplowitz were easy to miss. Caught in the no-man's land between administrators and teachers, counselors in many schools have a limited, little-understood role. They're neither in charge of big budgets nor directly involved with classroom academics. They don't teach anyone geometry and aren't really anyone's boss. They handle lots of scheduling complaints and deal with transcripts and grades—usually assigned so many students that there's almost no chance for them to develop individual relationships. In many schools they're perceived as little more than glorified clerks—essential to the operation of the school but not particularly prominent or important.

The lack of attention suited Kaplowitz just fine. One of two counselors assigned to work with the black shirts, she liked staying in the background as much as possible. She didn't give speeches at faculty meetings. She didn't like talking to the press. She just went about her business, which was helping schedule kids and make sure they had the right classes to graduate. But the kids loved her. Miss K's tiny cubicle was the farthest to the left in the counseling office located next to the administrative office where Cubias and Moody had desks. Her area was full of paper clutter, pictures of students, bright red University of Maryland paraphernalia, and students—lots and lots of students. There was a near-constant parade of them in and around her crowded office space. They talked with her about their classes and their problems. They stayed in her cubicle checking text messages while she talked to other students. Sometimes there were so many students in the counseling office that Cubias had to go in and tell them to keep it down; the noise was disturbing nearby classrooms. But it was worth it. Kaplowitz kept kids from dropping out. She convinced parents not to withdraw their children unnecessarily. She put things simply and directly in ways the kids appreciated: "Just do the notebook," she told one of the kids who needed to pass biology. "That's all he cares about." Some of the kids started calling her "Obama" for her constant repetition of the mantra, "Yes, you can." Her office was an informal study hall, a floating, open-air forum to talk about teachers, grades, parents, and—most of all—graduation.

Kaplowitz had first met David near the start of the school year, when the boy had (like several others) told her how beautiful she was and half-jokingly asked her out. Kaplowitz deflected the come-on; she knew that the kids were just showing off in front of their friends. Then halfway into the year, David started soliciting her help. Though not yet completely soured on David, Moody was happy to pass him along. Maybe she would have better luck. Now, Kaplowitz was calling to wake David in the mornings, picking him up before school, and giving him a ride home. She would get him a uniform shirt if he didn't have one, persuade his teachers to give him extra chances, and convince him to do makeup work. He was more responsive to Kaplowitz than he had been to anyone else. He wasn't actually failing all of his classes, and could easily catch up and redo assignments if needed. He had only forty minutes of detention time next to his name—a relatively small amount by Locke standards. Even more significant, thought Kaplowitz, David was trying to make good in the classes where he had been struggling.

A couple of hours after her confrontation with Moody, Kaplowitz stood in the darkness of Hobbs Hall, supervising a handful of kids who were on lunch detention.

The room was hot even though there were no lights on—no one could find the special key needed to turn them on. One of the students played the piano in the corner. The other kids sat silent in fold-up chairs. Moody was outside in the covered eating area, standing on a picnic table and hustling kids through the lunch line as he always did. You could hear his loud voice telling kids to keep the line straight. David was still not on campus.

"Sometimes I think I'm crazy," she said. "But with his current classes and ten credits he could actually graduate."

Kaplowitz knew that Moody cared about the kids, but also knew that he saw the situation differently. He was dealing with David's behavior and demeanor rather than his long-term potential.

"He's annoying and disrespectful," said Kaplowitz. "I get it."

But at this point she wasn't sure there was anything more she could do to help David. Moody thought he should be expelled. Cubias seemed to agree. For once, Kaplowitz wasn't sure what to do. She knew she was capable of falling into crazy relationships with kids, spending gobs of time with them and believing everything they said to her. She claimed to have been cured of that habit. "I don't do that anymore. Not since Alberto." But she'd never gone this far for a kid. She'd never had a fight like this. She didn't want to be in conflict with Moody and Cubias, her two closest allies in the school. She didn't want to go someplace new. She didn't want to lose. For a moment standing there in the darkness, Kaplowitz looked down and seemed unable to speak.

••

Friday morning, the day of prom, Cubias, Kaplowitz, and Moody still hadn't come to any agreement about what to do with David. They'd been trying to talk it out over the past three days, but had been stymied by interruptions and scheduling conflicts. Finally, they decided to sit down in the little-used conference room across from their offices and hash it out once and for all between the start of school and the midmorning break. Cubias and Moody sat on one side of the table, Moody in a blue polo shirt and Cubias in a bright orange one. Moody had printed out David's records and laid them in two neat rows on the table. On a small pad of paper, he'd listed other students who had been kicked out or nearly so—some of the most trouble-prone kids in the school. Across the hall, David sat in Kaplowitz's office, wearing a long T-shirt underneath his uniform and an earphone dangling from one ear. He didn't give any indication that he knew his fate was being decided across the hall (or that he cared either way). "Nobody has gotten away with as much as David," said Cubias. "Not Sammy or Alberto. Not even Ricky. We're talking about two fights; we're talking about suspicion of selling drugs, and all the rest."

"He says it to my face," said Moody. "'You're not going to catch me.'"

Kaplowitz and her counseling partner, Raquel Michel, sat on the other side of the table. Kaplowitz didn't need any paperwork, having memorized most of the details of David's schedule and class performance by this point. She emphasized how easily corrected David's grades were, and that he'd already signed up to take makeup in night school. He had only two Fs, in English and math, and was on his way to making up the work that would get him to a C or D.

"I know that you think he's manipulating me," said Kaplowitz. "But I don't feel that I'm being manipulated. I feel like I'm standing up for something that I believe in." She agreed that David needed to get to school on time, and stop coming to school high. She pointed out that David had never asked her for help, and claimed that she'd learned her lesson earlier in the year about kids who didn't respond to help. "I don't do this," she said, banging her keychain on the table. "I don't have time if it's not working. But I do feel like it is working."

"He works with us," said Michel. "He has been working with other kids in our office. That means something to me."

"It's not being late," said Cubias. "It's being late without the intent, even making the attempt, with the blatant disregard for school rules or for authority," said Cubias, voice high and scratchy as it always became when he was agitated. "He needs to learn that there are rules that you need to follow."

"He's talking loud, but he's not saying anything," said Moody.

Pretty soon it was clear that the four were stuck, repeating the same points over and over. They were green. All of them were under thirty-five and they had less than three years of administrative experience among them. They were making an enormously important decision largely without supervision from anyone else, without even any real system in place for making these decisions. Then the bell rang for break before anything was resolved. They all left to get to their supervision posts. Upstairs patrolling the second-floor hallway, Cubias didn't really have his heart in it anymore, despite the vehemence he'd expressed in front of Kaplowitz and Michel. He didn't want to leave Moody hanging, but his anger at David had faded over the course of the past couple of days. Cubias liked David and wanted to give him the benefit of the doubt if Kaplowitz was willing to fight for him. He also knew that Coleman had heard about the situation from Kaplowitz earlier in the week, and had thought expulsion might be an overreaction. And so, as lunchtime approached, Cubias broke the news to Moody that they were going to let David stay a little longer, under tight supervision, that the time to expel him had passed. "We should have done it earlier," said Cubias.

Moody didn't fight the decision, though he didn't agree with it, either. "I understood Miss K's position," he said. "But David knows where I'm coming from. Game recognizes game." With that, the issue was pretty much decided. It had been a nasty spat, but now it was over. The foursome met briefly to wrap things up and decide how to break the news to David. There were hugs and apologies and appreciations all around. By lunchtime, David had ditched the day's remaining classes to get himself ready for prom. Cubias left early, too, so he could get his hair slicked down and his outfit just right. "It's a ghetto thing, this prissiness," he said on his way out the door.

Back in his office, Moody settled into his never-ending paper-work. He hated to take prom away from anybody, but he bristled at the notion of David's being allowed to go. "Dude doesn't deserve to go to prom. I'm just saying. He doesn't deserve to participate in any activities other than graduation."

14

DRINKS AT PROM

A few hours later that day, it was time for the senior prom, which was being held at the Ebell Wilshire, an elegant 1920s-era event space tucked in near downtown Los Angeles. Far removed from the worn-out streets of Locke, the air seemed cooler, softer. Stone replaced cement. Trees and grass replaced fences and dirt.

It was a beautiful California night, dry and cool but not cold, with the smell of gardenia in the air. Locke students arrived dressed up beyond recognition, walking slowly up the steps to the main entrance. The boys wore vests and ties and shiny shoes, intricate designs stenciled (and even spray-painted) into their hair. The girls wore shiny dresses with elaborate cutouts. The kids were all beaming. They looked as though they were in a black-and-brown version of *Guys and Dolls*.

But of course, before entering, everyone had to be searched for contraband: boys in one line, girls in the other. The box on the table slowly filled with lighters and bottles of mouthwash. Once inside, the students passed into an enclosed garden complete with a fountain and garden chairs. There was a dining room, a room set up for karaoke, and a dance floor surrounded by massive speakers.

Prom wasn't just a big deal for Locke's five hundred seniors, those lucky few who had made it through the bad old days and were going to finish the year (even if not all of them graduated). This was also the first class to graduate from the "new" Locke. The local PBS station had just aired a segment about three of the school's seniors. Producers and cameramen were there, recording the event for a potential follow-up story. He showed up with his live-in girlfriend, a former Locke teacher who now worked at another Green Dot school nearby. Cubias wore a dark suit and shirt, and had some extra gel in his hair. He greeted kids and adults enthusiastically, and flitted around checking out the different rooms. Not everyone on staff at Locke was excited about prom; many steered clear. But it seemed obvious that Cubias was going to enjoy the event and stay until the end. Prom was barely an hour old when he began to sing some Guns N' Roses songs with the kids in the karaoke room.

Kaplowitz was there, too, dressed up a little but not too much, pocket camera in hand. She dodged some overeager boys who wanted to give her a lap dance, danced with some of the teachers, and took pictures with some of her favorite students. The constant flow of students that seemed to swirl around her wherever she went was evidence that she must be doing something right. Later on in the evening, Cubias and Kaplowitz briefly caught each other's eye on the dance floor. Kaplowitz made pretend guns with her hands and shot in Cubias's direction. Pow. Pow. Pow.

David showed up with his slender girlfriend, another senior, wearing matching outfits of emerald and black. The couple sat alone most of the evening, making out a little bit in their chairs during dinner and then watching the dancing in the room next door. Later on in the night, they moved to chairs outside in the garden, David's dress shirt now untucked. Occasionally, he would go inside and circle around the edge of the dance floor before returning outside.

Moody was there, too, but he didn't show up in his usual shirt and tie and he didn't stay long. He didn't grab a plate of food, join the kids on the dance floor, or take pictures with his favorite students—some of them wearing outfits that he had helped buy. He didn't even show off some of his old-school dance moves. Wearing the same jeans, polo shirt, and tennis shoes he'd had on at work, he stood near the entrance for a few minutes and watched the kids mingle. He was gone before dusk turned to night.

Prom ended promptly at midnight, seemingly without any major incident. There was some grumbling from the kids (about the choice of king and queen and the mix of music played by the DJ) and some complaining from the adults (about the blank-faced front-to-back grinding that the kids considered normal dancing). At the end, adults handed out taxicab vouchers to kids, knowing that many would continue celebrating until the early morning hours. ("It's a coupon," explained Kaplowitz to the confused-looking kids holding slips of paper.)

••

The Monday morning after prom, everyone was back at his or her usual spots—Moody outside at the gate, Cubias getting things ready inside. A tight-faced Kaplowitz made an unusual appearance on the street, walking out the gate past Moody holding a black uniform shirt in one hand. Neither she nor Moody acknowledged each other. The Monday after he'd almost been kicked out of school, David was once again late and didn't have the uniform shirt he'd need to gain entrance to the school. Kaplowitz was out looking for him. Eventually she found him and got him to come on campus. But once upstairs in class, David seemed more interested in the music on his oversized silver headphones than on anything the math teacher had to say. He spent most of the time with his chair turned away from the front of the room, looking around at kids behind him. He leaned back in his chair, twisted around to see whose attention he could grab. He drew on his binder and crumpled paper into a ball before shooting it toward the wastebasket.

"There's no in between with some kids," said Avila, his math teacher. "We've been on him the whole year."

"He's been tardy twice already today," said Moody a little bit later.

"He's very lucky they let him back," said one of his teachers.

Kaplowitz checked in on him a couple of times during the day to make sure David was still in class. The sound of her heels clicking on the linoleum hallway floors would grow in volume, then she'd be there at the doorway peeking in for a few seconds.

••

In the meantime, everyone else on campus was talking about what had happened at prom. But it wasn't anything tragic, and it wasn't students who were the culprits. It was staff. One of the young teachers who had helped organize the event had snuck a bottle of alcohol and some mixers into the chaperone room where teachers left their coats. Not having eaten all day, she and another teacher had been tipsy by the end of the night. Their incapacitated state hadn't been obvious to everyone, but it hadn't gone entirely unnoticed either. Some kids said that one of the teachers had slurred her words in announcing the king and queen of prom. The other, it was rumored, had thrown up in the parking lot after the event. Later that Monday, one of the two teachers, a young first-year teacher from the South, smiled and shook her head, embarrassed about what had happened. But she didn't seem horribly worried about the consequences.

A couple more days passed, and it seemed as though the flurry of attention might die out as quickly as it had flared up. On Wednesday morning during the weekly faculty meeting, nobody brought up what had happened even in passing. But then, shortly after the faculty meeting, Cubias got a call from Coleman to come to her office. There was nothing unusual about that—Coleman and Cubias talked all the time. But when Cubias arrived, Coleman asked everyone else who was there to give them a minute to talk alone.

"That's the first time *that's* happened," said Boulden, Cubias's counterpart on the white side.

Ten minutes later, Coleman's door opened. Her face was a bit flushed, but neither she nor Cubias said what had been discussed behind closed doors. Only later, when Cubias was about to go back into his office, did he acknowledge what had happened earlier behind closed doors in Coleman's office.

"She thinks I had a drink at prom," said Cubias, reaching down to pull at the doorstop keeping the main door open. Then, after a pause and a small smile and a cough, "Yeah, I did."

It wasn't just that he'd had a drink; he was the administrator in charge of closing the event, the most senior person in attendance after Coleman and Boulden left.

Cubias didn't come back to school the next day. The two young teachers were absent, too. But everyone knew that was for drinking, and that they were just being suspended temporarily. About Cubias there was no explanation. All of a sudden, He was gone. No one knew for how long, or if he'd be coming back.

15

SHOOTING ON SAN PEDRO

Standing at his post on the second floor of the main building just as school was about to let out for the day, security guard Marlon Byrd heard someone yell "shots fired" on his radio and started running down the stairs and out of the building.

It was the second week in May, a week after prom, a Friday, the second day since Cubias stopped showing up. Fridays were always the worst. The kids were antsy. School staff were a little worn down. There were always a few people who called in sick that day. There were three long class periods to get through, plus lunch and advisory. It had been a long week for everyone who had had to fill in for all the things Cubias usually did.

Racing downstairs, Byrd heard the last shot ring out as he scrambled out the front gate. The sounds—like a baseball bat hitting a metal street lamp—were coming from the corner of San Pedro and 111th Street, no more than a hundred feet from the main exit of the school, from which hundreds of Locke students were about to appear, heading home after the dismissal bell rang.

••

A few weeks before, sitting at a carnitas joint he used to go to as a kid, Cubias had been unconcerned about his future prospects with Green Dot. He thought the black shirts were better run than any of the other schools on campus and that his contributions to the turnaround effort made him nearly untouchable. True enough, he had been the poster boy for the Locke turnaround. But now, he'd been told to go home and stay there. He didn't know for how long, or if he'd even be able to come back. His friends didn't know anything—or wouldn't tell him. For someone who hated being off campus for even a moment, staying at home was torture—like being on some sort of indefinite house arrest. He promised himself he wouldn't resign or sign a nondisclosure agreement if they put one in front of him. He'd fight it if they tried to fire him.

••

Byrd didn't know if anyone had been hit. He was wearing an oversized blue Locke polo shirt and jeans rather than the usual uniform. Six-foot-one and 210 pounds, the twenty-seven-year-old had a couple of tattoos on his neck and a radio in his hand. Running down the street in his jeans and black gym shoes, he looked like an oversized kid.

This was the second time there'd been a shooting in the past six weeks. The month before, a student got shot on the way to school, just before the start of morning classes. Some kids had come up and asked him where he was from—a constant question among teens in the neighborhood. He said he was SouthLos, and one started firing. He was lucky it was just a .22 caliber handgun. But from the voices on the radio this was something bigger—more shots, maybe a bigger gun.

••

Back at the home office downtown, Green Dot bigwigs had spent the past few days trying to figure out what they should do about Cubias. They had fired principals before; that wasn't the problem. The joke was that Green Dot fired more administrators than teachers. Two other principals had left already that year. But most other schools weren't under the same kind of scrutiny as Locke. And Cubias was important to the school's success, both practically and symbolically. If Green Dot fired Cubias, there would almost certainly be an uproar on campus, and public attention just weeks before graduation. They talked to Coleman about what she thought was best for the school. They called a few other districts to see what was usually done in similar situations. "What an idiot," said one of the Green Dot staff downtown. "What was he thinking?"

••

Reaching the corner of 111th and San Pedro, Byrd saw a heavyset Latino boy in a white shirt running away from the school and then left onto 111th Place, the residential street just south of the school. There was a hole in the front windshield of a blue car parked at the corner, where the shots had been fired. The car belonged to a Locke parent who had been waiting in her car for her son to get out of school. She'd unknowingly parked in front a known gang hangout and barely missed being hit when a teenager from another gang rode up on his bicycle, and the teen Byrd was now chasing started shooting. Byrd tried to keep the shooter in sight. Two uniformed security guards ran behind him.

••

Over the past year, Green Dot had pushed aside a handful of Locke staff who'd been instrumental to the conversion. They'd moved former English teacher Bruce Smith to a job at the home office that would last just over a year. Former Locke principal Frank Wells was at that very moment searching up and down the state of California for work—and not finding any. "You begin to question yourself," said Wells about his fruitless job search. The third original Green Dot supporter from Locke, science teacher Vanessa Morris, had announced her resignation as principal from one of the Locke schools in February. Although Cubias had done nothing illegal, he had reason to feel particularly vulnerable. Permanent legal residents since a Reagan-era amnesty in the 1980s, he and his family had started out in the United States as undocumented immigrants. His younger brother, Hermes, had been involuntarily deported three years before under the Patriot Act, sent back to a country (El Salvador) he hadn't known since childhood, leaving behind a son whom Cubias was now helping raise.

••

Sitting in their patrol car outside the school, officers Terry and Joyce started seeing hundreds of kids running down 111th Street. Turning the corner in their squad car, they saw Byrd chasing the shooter, who first tried to hide behind a group of kids walking home and then, having been spotted with the gun still in his hand, slipped into a backyard on 111th Place, where he was cornered. The officers crouched behind their squad car, telling everyone to get back. Joyce had a shotgun in his hands; Terry had his white-handled automatic out of its holster.

Back at the school, there was confusion but not a lot of panic. Kids didn't make it this far in this neighborhood without having been around a fair number of shootings.

"No one got shot," blared a voice over one of the school megaphones.

It was one of the counselors standing in front of the school reporting back onto campus.

"I repeat. No one got shot."

"Then why you keeping us here?" asked one of the students.

For school administrators, the shooting couldn't have happened at a more jumbled time of day. School was just letting out. Half the kids were already off campus, heading home, but a few hundred were still there. Lockdowns had been few and far between in recent months, and there was no specific procedure for locking down the school after classes were dismissed. Should they try to keep the remaining students on campus, or get them out of the area as soon as possible? Was the danger ongoing, or had the shooter been apprehended? No one seemed to know. Unable to reach the school police on the radio, Coleman walked off campus and down the street, looking for someone to tell her what was going on. Burnett tried to keep up in her high heels.

••

Why did Cubias drink at prom? There were a hundred possible explanations, none of them entirely satisfactory. He was going through a challenging, difficult year, a trial by fire that had many times pushed him as far as he could go. He was just a few months out of the classroom and not yet used to being a supervisor whose responsibilities extended beyond his own individual actions. Or, maybe, Cubias was just nervous. He wasn't nearly as confident as he appeared to be. No one really knew—not even Cubias.

••

By the time Coleman got out to 111th Place and San Pedro, it was all over. There were police cars at both ends of 111th Place, officers waving traffic off. The canine unit had finally arrived and flushed the gunman out of his hiding place. A few minutes later, officers were able to retrieve the gun that had been dumped a few feet away. Some bystanders stood and watched; others barely gave it a glance. First there was one blue police helicopter circling low overhead, then there were two. The mother whose car windshield had been shot out was reunited with her son, a sophomore on the white side. He and his mother walked down San Pedro, leaving the car where it was. Officers Terry and Joyce apologized to Coleman for not letting her know what to do with her students. She radioed back to the school that the coast was clear. No more than two hours later, Locke held its annual sports banquet. A nonlethal ghetto school shooting taking place on a busy news day, the incident wasn't reported in the press.

••

A few days later, word got out that Cubias had been suspended and docked two weeks' pay but would keep his job. His colleagues had been divided over what the appropriate punishment would be, but no one seemed to think he should have been fired, (and in practical terms they couldn't really afford to lose him). Cubias was relieved that he hadn't gotten sacked, and perfectly fine with losing pay. He knew that he'd lost a lot of respect among teachers and even students, and that Green Dot would look at him differently going forward. Fearful of the reaction he would receive upon his return to campus, he joked that maybe he should rent a dunk tank and let people throw softballs at him to get their frustrations out.

"'Dunk the Jerk' is what they should call it," he said.

16

THE *NEW YORKER*

In May, the *New Yorker* published an article about Steve Barr called "The Instigator."

The turnaround attempt had already been covered by NPR's Claudio Sanchez and featured by Sam Dillon of the *New York Times*. There was a Harvard Business School case study. Green Dot had been mentioned in the *Los Angeles Times* too many times to count. "The role of the media cannot be overplayed here," said a Los Angeles media expert.

But this largely complimentary article was Green Dot's biggest, most prestigious coverage to date. A lengthy feature in the magazine's annual "innovation" issue, it described the effort to fix Locke as having been difficult but largely successful, and conveyed the message that Green Dot was on the move: "We're being asked, 'Could you guys do five schools in L.A. next year? Could you expand beyond L.A.?'" said Barr in the *New Yorker* magazine. "If you'd asked a month ago, 'What about Green Dot America?' I would have said, 'No way.' But if this President wants to get after it I'm going to reconsider."

Barr talked about the possibility of doing a turnaround in Washington and perhaps even moving his family East. He'd been freed up since October, when he stepped down as CEO and passed day-to-day control over to Petruzzi. Now he could travel more, schmooze and develop connections and funding sources. Barr wasn't a manager in the traditional sense. He was a promoter, an agitator, a one-man ideas lab. He floated an ever-changing menu of notions, keeping those that made sense or gained traction and dropping those that didn't. Some actually became real—the twelve original Green Dot schools, the idea of a unionized charter school network, a parents union, the Locke transformation. Others—expanding TFA to 250,000 teachers, giving every kid an individual education plan, outlawing private schools—didn't fly (at least not right away). But Barr never ran out. "He is a walking, talking soundbite machine," wrote school reform advocate Joe Williams.

Now it seemed as though Green Dot had broken into education's big time, joining other much-touted organizations like KIPP, TFA, and the Harlem Children's Zone. It wasn't unreasonable to think that more prestigious coverage might be next—maybe *60 Minutes, The Oprah Winfrey Show*, or even *The Colbert Report*. Perhaps Secretary Duncan or even President Obama would come to the school's first graduation ceremony next month. It was all paying off—in recognition, at least.

••

Barr had known from the start that he was going to have to ruffle feathers and make sure that the media saw him doing it. Late to the school reform game, he needed to hype his work in order to get the money, rally talent, and motivate effort. It didn't hurt that he talked to reporters easily and often, hitting them with his tantalizing mix of edgy policy ideas and incredibly coarse language. He was friendly, gruff, and masculine while still seeming sensitive and intelligent. And he had a great personal story; he wasn't your typical child of privilege coming in to save the poor kids. His roller-coaster life story stood out on its own, and he wasn't afraid to talk about things that had happened to him and to his family. So it wasn't just fancy reformers and pencil-necked journalists to whom Barr appealed but also working-and middle-class families whose children were still in the public schools and whose relatives often worked in them. ("He's been down," said Miss Burnett about the *New Yorker* article. "But he's not afraid.") Barr made the blue-collar folks who'd put their hearts and souls into teaching feel more at home with a "reformer" than anyone had in a long time, while still appealing to the reformy types. Indeed, it wouldn't be long before book agents were approaching him about writing a memoir.

The publicity had certainly helped in the fundraising department; Green Dot raised $67 million over just nine years. But the rising wave of publicity brought with it a series of ever-growing dangers. Former Locke teachers didn't like hearing that their school had been "taken over." Home office staff worried about the suggestion in the *New Yorker* article that Green Dot had a "mole" in the district. The superintendent and the mayor didn't like finding out that Barr was still talking about "blowing up" the district with a citywide Armageddon plan to siphon students away from district schools. The Obama administration's education team was surprised to read that Green Dot was going nationwide—with their support. School officials in Washington DC weren't expecting Barr to talk about Green Dot taking over a school, which was at the time only in the discussion stages.

Most problematically for Green Dot, the *New Yorker* article emphasized Barr's role above all others, as if Barr were single-handedly running all of Green Dot's schools and himself teaching the kids at Locke. "Green Dot is six hundred people who all work their asses off, but the press aggrandizes one guy over everyone else," said Petruzzi, now the CEO of Green Dot. Barr's constant presence in the papers also rankled other school reform organizations, many of which had been around longer than Green Dot. His brash pronouncements jarred relationships and upset stakeholders. This was the downside of all the press that had been generated—hurt feelings, unrealistic expectations, and worn relationships within Green Dot and among school reform groups in the city, plus the danger that Barr could become overexposed and caricatured.

"Everybody's looking for him to fail," said one observer.

At a certain point, talking all the time seemed to become tiresome even for Barr. He showed up on campus once or twice a month, usually unannounced, to show VIPs around. He would give his tour, perch on his favorite corner in the quad, and tell his stories about what Locke used to be like and how much it had changed. He repeated the same spiel, like a candidate giving his campaign trail stump speech. "I've got like twenty stories I tell, and I tell them over and over." Sometimes he looked bored at events, idling until it was time for him to speak. At times awkward and insecure, he belittled others' accomplishments, jutted his top row of teeth out over his bottom lip when he was nervous or angry, and looked uncomfortable in a suit and tie no matter how many times he put one on.

••

Not too long after the *New Yorker* article came out, a trio of Green Dot managers drove up from downtown LA to a hotel in nearby Pasadena and presented the preliminary results from their first year at Locke at an annual conference of education hotshots. There were some positive findings to report—lower dropout rates, higher attendance. But the Green Dot folks were candid about what remained to be done at Locke, repeatedly pointing out that they hadn't "cracked the nut" of fixing failing schools.

"We're not there yet," said Cristina de Jesus, one of Green Dot's founding principals and chief academic officer. "People expect change, and they expect it quickly, but this is really difficult work."

"[Barr] makes it sound so easy, but it's not," said Petruzzi. "There's not a lot of talent out there. We have to build a lot of stuff on our own. We're one of just three school operators in the nation who are doing this, and we have just seven months under our belts."

They were trying to walk things back, to put the genie back in the bottle, to lower expectations. But it was too late.

17

"WE DID IT, Y'ALL"

Usually nearly imperturbable, Coleman began graduation day as ticked off as anyone had seen her all year. Sitting behind her desk, she spoke in a low, flat voice into her walkie-talkie. "Coleman to Lieutenant Moore. Lieutenant Moore, can you and Mr. Goodman come to my office at your earliest convenience?" Then she waited.

It was June 24, and graduation for the first year of the new Locke was scheduled to begin just a few hours later. The hope was that there would be a record-setting number of seniors graduating, a smooth graduation ceremony, and an upbeat end to the year for everyone. Past graduations had been somewhat disorganized events, with parents crashing the gate and walking around out on the field among the blue-robed graduates during the middle of the ceremony. Coleman had spent weeks trying to plan and prepare for a good event—making sure the gates were staffed and that everyone knew the protocols for who got in and who didn't. But this morning she'd shown up before school and found none of the security guards at their posts.

It was a somewhat strange time to be celebrating. Just a few days before the July Fourth holiday, most other high schools were already finished. The economy was in shambles; teachers all over the city were losing their jobs. Over the past weekend, a wiry Locke student Johnny had been shot hanging out in front of his house with a friend and was in critical condition. One thing was sure, however: the press would be swarming the event. Public attention for so-called turnaround efforts like that at Locke had multiplied over the past twelve months, thanks in large part to President Obama's $3.4 billion effort to fix the nation's worst five thousand schools. Locke had become one of the most-watched school reform efforts in the nation, a test of whether failing schools could be fixed and whether charters—unionized or not—could be part of the solution. Camera crews from *Nightline* and the local PBS station would be there, as well as several local TV stations and print reporters. The morning's front page of the *Los Angeles Times* was covered with a giant picture of a mother kissing her smiling, blue-robed Locke graduate.

When Lt. Moore arrived in Coleman's office a few minutes later, Coleman gave him and his boss, Eddie Goodman, a good talking to; they hung their heads like chastened schoolboys and promised to be on the ball for the rest of the day. Done playing angry principal, Coleman pulled her cap and gown out of the square plastic bag it had been sitting in for the past few days. Maybe next year she'd have time to do a little ironing.

Things were a little more leisurely in the counseling office, where Kaplowitz was sitting at her desk checking e-mails while a student stood behind her, styling her thick brown hair. There were flowers from her boyfriend sitting in a vase next to her laptop. Just hours before graduation, she still wasn't done figuring out who was going to graduate. They wanted to reach four hundred, but didn't want to overstate the results and have to correct them later. Some kids would walk in the ceremony but wouldn't get a diploma. Some kids had enough credits but still hadn't passed the state exit exam. A small number of those who were still coming to school wouldn't be able to walk in the event at all. The dark rings under Kaplowitz's eyes revealed that she hadn't slept much the past couple of weeks. She'd been pushing to get as many seniors as possible to pass their classes, cajoling kids to do makeup work and negotiating with teachers to persuade them to accept late assignments, pushing teachers to let them pass. "I've been like a politician these last few days," Kaplowitz said. "I talk to the teachers on behalf of the kids. I go back to the kids and tell them what the teachers need." Kaplowitz became emotional—out of relief as well as pride—when she first found out that David passed enough of his classes and was going to participate in graduation. For his part, Cubias was pleased at the outcome. Moody still wasn't so sure. In the meantime, word had gotten out that Kaplowitz was being promoted to head counselor next year.

Behind the scenes, there was grumbling from some of the teachers about how many kids were graduating. As a charter, Green Dot enjoyed some wiggle room in determining who could participate in graduation and had decided that any senior who was within one or two classes of graduation could participate in the ceremony. The theory was that they would legitimately be done by the end of summer school and so could be counted as a 2009 graduate, and that it was a good thing to encourage as many kids as possible to push through and get as many credits as they could, rather than have them drop out at the thought of doing an extra semester in the fall. But many teachers had heard about this decision from kids and counselors before anyone told them officially. "We had to ask about it at a faculty meeting," said Sully. Under the previous regime, "If you failed English 12B, you weren't walking." For cynics like Sully, the reason was obvious. "They know it's going to be live on the national news, four hundred kids graduating from Locke."

The day was starting out sunny and blue-skied, with just a little breeze. Starting at about 3:00, teachers and students finally began gathering in the gym, while parents started arriving on campus and heading toward the football field where the ceremony was being held. There were staff and security at the gates, making sure that everyone who came in had a ticket (and had bags checked). Out on the football field, Cubias's childhood friend Jorge "George" Alvaron—now a clerk on the white side—chased one last stray dog off campus just before the parents arrived. For a time the dingy white-haired mutt wandered around exactly where the ceremony was going to be held. "I gotta get that dog," said Alvaron, who finally shooed the mutt out the gate.

Gathered in the gym, students and teachers milled about together waiting for the ceremony to begin. The long shiny robes made the students look older but made the teachers look younger. There hadn't been time to get teachers the hoods and colors that corresponded to their degrees, so it was decided that everyone—even newly minted college grads—got a cowl that signified an advanced degree of some sort.

For Cubias, the day was a whirlwind of greeting, being greeted, stopping for pictures, pulling kids close with a friendly hand behind their necks. Parents and recent graduates came up to say hello. Always the dandy, Cubias had put his long black hair back with a thin hair band similar to the kind that soccer players sometimes wear. He had an oversized pair of aviator sunglasses perched on his head, and a maroon-and-blue hood hanging off the back of his robe. "Damn, my hair looks good," he said.

Many of the teachers appeared to be in a celebratory mood, too. "This year went by so fast. I can't believe it's over already," said Leeya Shaked, a special education teacher who'd been at the old Locke. "I am definitely happy that I stayed." Newly-arrived drama teacher Monica Mayall was happy she'd stuck it out, too.

After an exhausting first semester, she felt as though the kids had started to put in a real effort and buy into the turnaround, and she had focused on helping get kids past the state graduation exam. "This school has a completely different vibe," she said about how the year ended. She credited Coleman for picking good people. Still, Mayall was planning on handing off her union duties. "Next year someone else can be the policeman." Social studies teacher Jeremy Zuniea had come out of the closet and started a LBGT support group. Even English teacher Maggie Bushek seemed relaxed. She'd taken a step back from the constant grind a couple of months before when a colleague told her one day after a particularly bad lesson that it looked as though she hated teaching. "This is so non-TFA," she said, "but I decided to accept the fact that there were going to be some things that I wasn't going to get to." Teachers weren't the only ones happy they'd ended up at Locke and stayed through the transition. A junior named Cassie described the fight that had gotten her transferred from another school to Locke as "the best fight I ever had."

Finally, just after 4:00, the music began, and students and teachers walked onto the red rubber track surrounding the football field and did a lap in front of the crowd in the bleachers. After circling the track, students lined up to go onstage and received their diplomas. Kaplowitz helped organize the line, making sure that the kids' names were pronounced correctly and matched with the faces of the students going up onto the stage. Cubias and Boulden handed out diplomas and exchanged hugs and big smiles with each of the students; there was a quick pose for the cameras with each—smile!—and then it was on to the next graduate. The students walked offstage and sat on white chairs arranged into a square in the middle of the football field. The group of graduates now sitting in white chairs looked small out there, an island of baby-blue gowns in a sea of grass. Camera crews and producers circled the kids whom they had chosen to profile. A security guard rode his bicycle in lazy circles around the red oval track.

Over on the sidelines stood young athletic director Stephen Minix, wearing a khaki summer suit, gym shoes, and white plastic sunglasses on his head. Also standing among the onlookers was Kerón, the football player who'd been pepper-sprayed by security guards earlier in the year, who was there to watch his girlfriend, Laurie, graduate. During the spring semester, Cubias had moved Kerón over to the white shirts, and then to the alternative program, but he was supposed to return to Big Locke and rejoin the football team for his last year. Officer Terry, the school police officer who'd arrested Kerón during the riot thirteen months before, was there, too. Officer Palacio had already left to go to another nearby high school. Former Locke English teacher Bruce Smith was also there in the crowd. He was still working at Green Dot headquarters but had the sense that he was going to be let go soon, as Wells had been the year before.

Gowned and wearing his slick black wraparound sunglasses, Moody began the formal part of the ceremony with a moving invocation that called on all of those assembled to watch out for the students from Locke. He asked everyone to rise and stretch their hands out toward the seated seniors, to protect and bless them. It was a symbolic laying on of hands, and an explicit reference to all the dangers and obstacles Locke kids faced, past and future. Up on the stage, Cubias briefly cried behind his sunglasses.

Now the sun was edging downward, shadowing the black-robed administrators on the stage and shining straight into the faces of the assembled seniors. Here and there, air horns bleated out from the crowd in the stands. Some students chattered among themselves, cracking jokes and commenting on the speakers in words too quiet to be heard by the teachers who sat at the end of each row or by the audience in the faraway stands. Others sat quietly, focused on the proceedings. Stepping up to the podium, Barr looked tall and strangely professorial in his round Harry Potter spectacles. His cowl was gold and light blue, and his robe had three felt bands on each sleeve. He'd just gotten back from another trip East the day before, during which Green Dot had finally signed a formal contract for its new school in New York City. The New York City school showed that the Green Dot model could work outside of Los Angeles and with a "real" union. Filmmaker Davis Guggenheim had been on hand to document the moment for a movie he was working on. The month before, Barr had testified in front of the House education committee—the first time he'd testified in front of Congress since the early 1990s.

Unlike at past Green Dot graduations, Barr didn't really know many of the Locke parents and teachers and kids he was addressing. There had been lots of trips and outside obligations during the year. The school was a long way off from Green Dot's downtown offices and Barr's home. Several of Locke's teachers said that Barr still didn't know their names despite having met him several times. The students didn't really know him, either, often confusing him with Kelly Hurley, another tall white guy from Green Dot who wasn't around all that much.

During his speech, Barr leaned sideways into the podium with one elbow and used the other arm to gesture. The late afternoon sun shone against the side of his face.

"How many of you are going to come back to change this neighborhood?" he asked. "Who will be the doctor that will cure the sick? There's a hand—I'm going to hold you to it. Who will represent those who need legal assistance?"

The audience responded with a smattering of applause.

"Who will be inspired by these young teachers and come back and teach? Come on, let's see some more hands."

He pushed the bridge of his round-framed glasses back up his nose.

"How many of you will come back and teach? More than you think."

"How many of you will register to vote and come back and be politically active? Come on, some of you had your hands up. Anyway, this is what it's going to take."

The wind picked up, blowing Barr's hair forward as though he was sitting in a convertible driving down the highway. He rubbed the back of his neck and tried to pat his hair back into place as best he could.

Finally, Barr wrapped it up: "I can't wait to look across the street in ten years and see who opens the first bookstore, café where poetry is read, organic grocery store so that all the families from Watts can have healthy food. Who will be the next congressman? Who will be the next mayor? These are the questions we ask, and that is the work. Help us fill this stadium with graduates. Help us fulfill the original purpose of Locke and bring hope to this neighborhood. You have started that track. Thank you, class of 2009."

"Thank *you*, Steve Barr," responded a voice from among the students.

Perhaps the most memorable remarks of the day came from a very nervous Donna Taylor, the valedictorian for Locke 4—the green shirts—and the first in her family to graduate from high school.

"Some say we can't handle our business," said Donna, who wore giant wraparound sunglasses and was only able to complete her speech with the help of a steady stream of encouraging remarks from students and teachers on the stage. "They just don't understand." Voice growing stronger as she went, Donna waved a hand in the air. "We made it. We did it, y'all. Forget the haters. Let's go. We did it."

At the end of the long event, the graduates threw their mortarboards in the air, and Vivaldi blared out of the PA system. Students and their families mingled and took pictures out on the field and in the quad. The hot, sunny day had turned into a cool early evening. A couple of kids from the band played a bit of mariachi music as they walked from the field into the quad. Some of Miss K's kids waited for her to drive them home. There was a big hug between Barr and Cubias, who walked a couple of steps with their arms around each other before separating. It was late, however, so no one stayed too long. Kids and families headed off to restaurants and parties. Coleman rode away in her big shiny pickup, with Cubias not far behind in his dusty blue minivan. The next day he would be stuck in his office finishing evaluations, while Kaplowitz would be in her office ringing a bell whenever a senior came in and it was clear that he or she'd graduated. A close double-overtime basketball game between the guards and staff would be marred by some questionable calls from Lt. Moore—now mysteriously promoted to Commander. During the final faculty meeting, Coleman would get an extended standing ovation from her staff—including several who'd initially questioned her appointment. Then it was all over, the first year of the new Locke was done.

PART THREE

BECOMING A SCHOOL

18

THE NEW FACE
OF GREEN DOT

"I dare you to fucking look at my numbers," said Green Dot CEO Marco Petruzzi, sitting at a small round conference table in his tidy office and rattling off a series of statistics. In Green Dot's first year at Locke, Petruzzi would tell anyone who'd listen, attendance was up from 78 percent to 89 percent, test scores nudged upward despite a 38 percent increase in the number of students being taught, the graduation rate rose by 15 percentage points, and suspensions due to violent incidents were down by 50 percent. The torrent of figures went on. "It's an incredibly less violent campus than it was before," said Petruzzi, who liked to keep his chair pulled up close to the edge of the table.

But in the days and weeks after graduation, Petruzzi's view of things was matched by an opposing view: disappointment. Attendance rates were up. Discipline infractions were down. The new school had improved relationships with parents, enhanced kids' sense of being cared for, and helped a bunch of seniors get across the finish line and make it out of school. But the passing rates on the state exit exam had barely budged for sophomores. The state exam scores weren't that much better than previous years, either. They'd actually gone down slightly. A lot of kids still failed to get caught up on their credits and still fell through the cracks—flunking classes, attending only occasionally. Advanced Placement scores came back in July and were "nothing to brag about," according to Bruce Smith, the former AP English teacher. "Great job, guys," said Kevin Sully, the resident critic on the English faculty. "No one got killed on campus this year." Sully still thought that Green Dot should be at Locke. "I just wish they'd done it right." The local newspaper seemed to go along with Sully's glass-half-empty assessment: "Locke is much changed from what it was a year ago, but it is not transformed," proclaimed an editorial in the *Los Angeles Times*. "The bloom is off the rose," said charter school guru Greg Richmond. "Locke wasn't perfect."

Indeed, Green Dot's first year at Locke hadn't produced any miraculous results.

••

Originally an unpaid board member, Petruzzi left his partnership at Bain & Company to become COO of Green Dot in January 2007 and then quietly succeeded Barr as CEO in October 2008. In some ways, the leadership transition had started taking place more than a year and a half before that, during the spring and summer of 2007 when Green Dot was pushing to win control over Locke. But as far as most people were concerned, Barr was still Green Dot, and Green Dot was still Barr. Almost a year into his tenure, few outside the organization really understood that Petruzzi was now in charge of Green Dot.

Tall and slender with white hair, Petruzzi looked like a doctor or maybe a priest on a network TV show. His striped dress shirts were untucked but pressed, and his shirtsleeves were rolled neatly up his slender forearms. His accent was hard to place—it sounded Canadian to some, or maybe Scandinavian. He touched his lips with two long fingers when waiting to make a point or pondering a question. Four years younger than Barr, Petruzzi exhibited a business-world formality and language that sometimes made him seem older. He didn't talk about people; he talked about "talent." He didn't talk about getting things done; he talked about "execution." His explanations usually strung big gobs of details and figures together. (He was also bluntly honest. Green Dot's first year of Locke could have been a nightmare, Petruzzi readily admitted. "Easily.")

There were many who admired Petruzzi's abilities and saw great promise in what he would do to move Green Dot forward. He was an "organizational genius," according to one board member. ("I know how to plan like crazy," was how Petruzzi put it.) "He's calm, cool, collected, and very methodical—typical Bain," said Tom Vander Ark, the former executive director of education for the Bill & Melinda Gates Foundation. "He's what they need to get better and scale." Others worried that Petruzzi wasn't charismatic or compelling enough—that he came off as too much of a technocrat.

Underneath the surface there were some obvious similarities with Barr. Petruzzi was an ambitious, self-made man who came to school reform through a circuitous route. He shared Barr's desire for Green Dot to do "another Locke"—to repeat the transformation effort that they'd begun at Locke at another school—to grow. His first major project with Green Dot had been the Bain & Company plan that laid out how Green Dot could do it. And—usually in private—Petruzzi could be just as stubborn and temperamental and foulmouthed as Barr.

Born and raised in Italy, Petruzzi lived in Mexico for seven years while his father, a blue-collar textile worker, worked as a factory supervisor there. After a relatively brief return to Italy, Petruzzi arrived in the United States for an international exchange program and never went back. He was sent to Unionville, Tennessee (population one hundred), for his senior year of high school. A year later, he enrolled as an engineering major at Columbia University, from which he received both a BA and an MBA. He had fifteen years of consulting experience and had been a partner at Bain & Company, during which he lived all over the world. He now lived in Venice with his school-age children and his Brazilian-born wife. It was a whole new world for him.

During the time period in which they were both with the organization, Green Dot had benefited from Barr and Petruzzi's complementary skill sets. But from the start there had been tensions between these two strong personalities working in close proximity, one getting nearly all the public credit and the other working the shadows. Where Barr focused on ideas, Petruzzi focused on implementation. Where Barr pushed large-scale reforms that went far beyond Green Dot's immediate commitments, Petruzzi focused on running and improving the existing network of Green Dot schools. Where Barr could be combative and critical in public, Petruzzi politely praised his counterparts in other organizations. Where Barr loved the spotlight, Petruzzi insisted on sharing it. Green Dot raised tens of millions in funding over the years, but "it wasn't anything Steve did alone," Petruzzi said. "It was a powerful proposal put together by a team that worked amazingly hard." The same was true for the Locke takeover, according to Petruzzi. And there was never any serious consideration of Green Dot going national during the spring of 2009, either. "That was just Steve," said Petruzzi, who had since his arrival at Green Dot been dismayed at how many times he had to swoop in and clean up one of Barr's messes or make good on one of his unanticipated commitments. Petruzzi credited Barr as a great ideas man but chafed at the notion that merely thinking something up was somehow more important than making it happen.

Petruzzi's theme was that running schools was challenging work—that it took a tremendous amount of effort by a host of smart people working together. It could be done—Green Dot was doing it—but there was nothing quick or easy or dramatic about it. No single person could get done what really required a concerted effort from a dedicated team, and any illusions to the contrary would be quickly shattered.

"For us, an idea is just 1 percent of the job," said Petruzzi. "Ninety-nine percent is execution."

Under Petruzzi, Green Dot tried to limit distractions and keep focus internally on the schools it was already running. Limiting distractions sometimes meant declining press opportunities, too. When the producers for *Waiting for "Superman"* proposed involving Locke students in a segment in which they would pull T-shirts out of a box to find out if they were going to jail, working a job, or going to college, Petruzzi's chief academic officer responded, "No, we're not doing that."

Now firmly in control, Petruzzi was also trying to adapt Green Dot to the ever-evolving education environment and make sure Green Dot would last. He hired new staff, cut spending, and, where necessary, let people go. He revamped internal operations, strengthened the educational supports for the schools, and made sure that the organization had enough money coming in. On the academic front—the area on which Green Dot would ultimately be judged—Petruzzi felt a particular urgency. Green Dot didn't work with a "tight" instructional model like KIPP's, where a visitor would see numerous similarities—class schedules, math lessons, "Work Hard, Be Nice" signs on the walls—from one location to the next. Some Green Dot schools offered intensive remediation and support; others left such interventions up to each teacher. Some teachers taught one book a year; others made it through a slew of them. A variety of different math textbooks were being used. Green Dot had grown quickly based on a teacher-led model, and was only now building, testing, and piloting a systemwide instructional model. The academic results for individual Green Dot schools were all over the place. Though they outperformed their district counterparts, as of 2009, not a single Green Dot school had reached the target score of 800 on its state report card, and several were not making the kind of yearly progress that was expected. "We went seven years without an education team," said Petruzzi. "We've been playing catch up." Under Petruzzi, Green Dot was going to try to bring coherence and order to a network of disparate charter schools—developing and standardizing systems that had emerged haphazardly over the past ten years. "Autonomy isn't 'whatever the hell I want to do,'" said Petruzzi.

Although there hadn't been much Petruzzi could do during Locke's first year, by the second year, the opportunity and the need were both there. Green Dot now had nineteen schools, approximately eighty-three hundred students, and nearly seven hundred employees, but for 2009–2010 Green Dot was opening just one new school—a small career technical school. It wasn't growing at breakneck speed anymore. Now Petruzzi's education team could begin what he politely called "hard conversations" at several of the schools. New intervention programs were going to be piloted for possible use. Petruzzi described the process as Green Dot's "finding its true North"—a 5 percent shift, he said. Not everyone at the school level anticipated these changes eagerly, and Petruzzi knew that bringing order to Green Dot would in some ways be as difficult a challenge as opening slews of new schools each year. "We don't want to devolve into something prescriptive or top down," said Petruzzi. "We don't want to lose our DNA." Indeed, the urge to standardize and centralize is a strong one, and the academic focus under Petruzzi wasn't going to be any touchy-feely kind of thing that teachers and principals might welcome. Petruzzi and his team were focused squarely on improving academic performance, as measured by test scores. It was about data, interventions, and supports—a consultant's version of academics rather than a teacher's. Petruzzi felt that there was no more time to reinvent the wheel—no more time to assume that there was method to the madness. Slowly but surely, Green Dot was turning into a more traditional charter management organization: providing services, starting schools, and focusing on the difficult tasks of growing and improving schools on a day-to-day basis. Implementation was replacing innovation, though most of the effects had yet to be felt at Locke.

At the same time, Petruzzi also had to convince the academic team and the board to push ahead with doing another turnaround. Growth was Green Dot's lifeblood just as it is for any other organization. It's what paid for the central office staff to support the schools, serve more kids, and keep up the pressure on the district to do better. So, during the fall and winter of 2008–2009, Petruzzi carefully crafted a plan to do a second Locke-style transformation starting in 2010–2011 and a third the year after that. His plan won approval from the board in March.

Whether Petruzzi's plan would succeed was something no one knew. The economy was worsening. The Gates Foundation wasn't going to give Green Dot funding for a second turnaround. Several other big philanthropies were turning away from charter expansion initiatives after years of funding them. History was littered with start-ups that seemed promising during the first few years but didn't make it past a decade. "This is where most start-ups fail," Petruzzi said.

19

BARR STEPS DOWN

Barr wasn't on campus or in the office all that much during the summer after Locke's first year or during the start of its second. When he wasn't traveling to Washington or New York, he spent most of his time working from his home in Silver Lake. He had a big deck off the second floor where he liked to work and a downstairs study where he kept a blown-up version of the illustration that had accompanied the *New Yorker* article showing him standing in front of Locke, arms crossed. What was he up to? Why wasn't he around?

In early July, just a few weeks after graduation, Green Dot filed its 990 form for the previous tax year. Posted online, 990s are IRS reports required for nonprofit organizations; they are usually pretty unremarkable. But this particular one contained an unusual disclosure about the period of January 2004 through September 2007: almost $51,000 in "unreimbursable" business expenses paid to Barr. During three hectic years when Green Dot had grown enormously, Barr had expensed and been reimbursed for $50,866 in items that were, according to the small note included in the 990 form, "either not reimbursable in nature, or were insufficiently substantiated or documented to qualify for reimbursement."

The reimbursement issue wasn't news within Green Dot. The findings were the result of an audit commissioned at Petruzzi's request nearly two years before, in 2007. The news wasn't entirely new outside Green Dot, either. Unspecified rumors about Barr's spending habits had started circulating among a small circle of education watchers during the previous winter and spring. The only thing that was new was that now there was an official admission posted online for everyone to see. Barr and those at the home office downtown waited gingerly to see if anyone would notice. For a long while, no one did.

According to Barr, it was he who suggested the look into the expenses issue in the first place—as a precautionary measure. Nonprofits like Green Dot are prohibited from purchasing liquor with public funds. He'd heard about another charter network getting in trouble for covering the costs of teacher happy hours. "I said, 'Let's get ourselves organized like real grown-ups,'" said Barr. The misspending was just the by-product of the organization having grown so quickly in such a short amount of time, he said. Barr took Green Dot teachers out once or twice a year, sometimes inviting interested outsiders to join. He met them at nearby watering holes and picked up the tab. "It's a drinking culture," he said. "You gotta drink with them."

In late October, two years after the audit was commissioned and nearly four months after the information was filed publicly, the news finally gained a small measure of notice. An eagle-eyed education blogger named Kenneth Libby read Green Dot's 990 form, noticed the item about the overspending, and, the day before Halloween, posted an entry titled "How'd Steve Barr Spend $50,866?"

No one who knew Barr really thought he'd been systematically embezzling. He still drove his decade-old police cruiser and wore the same three suits over and over. People just thought he'd been doing something extremely careless. After a flurry of postings on education blogs, the issue seemed to die down.

Then on a Friday afternoon the week before Thanksgiving—less than a month later—things got even stranger. Local NPR affiliate KPCC radio posted a brief news story with the startling headline, "Green Dot Public Schools Chairman Steve Barr steps down." Just a few days before, he had been sitting at an upscale bar overlooking Grand Central Station in New York City, seemingly unworried about the reimbursement issue and full of ideas about what his next capers would be. Now it was being reported that he was leaving Green Dot. There was no official press release. For several long hours, neither Green Dot nor its public relations firm nor Barr issued any sort of explanation or responded to e-mails. I hastily posted a blog entry about the sudden move. The morning after, Green Dot said that Barr was merely stepping down from being chairman. He would remain on the board and serve on the executive committee. There was no connection to the note in the 990, according to Barr, who described the events as "a coincidence of timing."

But then, December 2, the *Los Angeles Times* reported that it wasn't just poor record keeping and the occasional bar tab that were at issue. Barr's successor as chairman, education school dean Shane Martin, described "isolated instances of expenses that were more extravagant than they needed to be for a nonprofit." Barr also admitted to using his Green Dot credit card for personal expenses one or two times—emergency surgery on his wife's dog and three nights of vacation—but "paid it back the next day."

And there was no widespread problem, said Martin, just a very small handful of instances. Barr was well on his way to repaying the organization and had admitted that his recordkeeping had been poor.

Behind the scenes, board members and staff debated for nearly a week over whether or not to give the *Times* the full audit and let the consequences fall as they may. (Asked about the reimbursement mess, Petruzzi would only say, "I've been asked not to talk about this by the board.") The most immediate problem for Barr and for Green Dot was dealing with the perception that they were in it for the money. There is a long, sad history in education of people taking money meant for poor children and wasting it or using it for their own purposes. Charter schools are no better or worse. But some educators viewed charter schools—even ones run by non-profit organizations—as a form of "privatization." And Barr had spent years slamming the teachers union and the district for spending money "like drunken pirates." A few days after the *Times* story ran, Green Dot finally released a summary version of the audit to the paper. The paper's editorial page was unmoved. "The public shouldn't have to beg for answers about how its money is spent or be grateful for getting them," it declared.

At every step of the way, Barr and Green Dot board president Shane Martin asserted that the reimbursement issue had nothing to do with Barr's change in status within the organization. "That's not where the board was," said Martin. Barr's next move was to take a more evangelical, advisory role and create a new spinoff initiative called Green Dot America. He'd always hoped to make a bigger mark on school reform than any single charter management organization could hope to do. His strengths were his persuasive muscle and energizing effect on parents and teachers, his powerful sense of mission and spirit. Now, according to Martin and others, Barr was just going back to his roots in political activism and advocacy. The move made perfect sense—it just wasn't clear why Barr needed to leave Green Dot to do it.

Conflicts and disputes within organizations or among allies aren't all that uncommon in education or any other endeavor, though they only occasionally receive attention. In November 2009, for example, veteran education journalist Tom Toch removed his name from a report he'd written because a good deal of his research had been edited out—by the organization he had cofounded and then departed. On and off between 2008 and 2010, then Washington DC schools chief Michelle Rhee criticized the Obama education agenda as being weak and watered down. (At one point Education Secretary Arne Duncan fired back with the quip, "You can't fire your way to the top"—a swipe at Rhee's controversial dismissal of scores of teachers.) But lots of other organizations—think TFA—had founders who stayed on as CEO as long as two decades, and many others—think *Huffington Post*—had founders who functioned as the public face of the organization, bringing in money and developing new ideas while others took care of operations.

To be sure, Barr had over the years chronically said or done things controversial enough that his colleagues and allies had to paper over whatever mess had been created. He was famously impulsive. (Teachers union president Randi Weingarten liked to tell the story about how Barr agreed to open a Green Dot school in New York City as soon as she proposed it. "Don't you want to think about it?" she remembered asking him.) He didn't come to the office regularly, attend senior staff meetings, or respond to work e-mails and calls, some said. ("Too much like real work for him," quipped Coleman when he stepped down as CEO the year before.) Even some of his strongest allies worried that his flamboyant personality made him easy to stereotype. "At times even Steve falls into his own caricature," said longtime friend and former district board member Caprice Young. Personality may have played a part, too. Even after the immediate public relations crisis was averted, faces tightened among some Green Dot staffers when Barr's name was mentioned. Warm and generous as he could be in public, Barr sometimes lapsed into behavior that seemed critical and off-putting to some of those who had worked with him. "How do you alienate everyone in the organization you started?" said someone closely familiar with Green Dot's home office who did not wish to be identified. "At the end of the day, he was a kind of self-absorbed dick."

According to Martin, Barr was simply responding to ideas and opportunities outside the office even if no one else at headquarters knew what was going on. Having Barr chair the board didn't work out because of how closely the district was monitoring Green Dot's efforts and how quickly it demanded formal decisions. According to Barr, he'd stopped coming in to the office to give Petruzzi room to operate. "I wanted this guy to have his own thing," he said. If he had rubbed people the wrong way or worked them too hard for too long, well, that was the price of growing so quickly and getting so much done. "It's a hard fucking job."

Confident as he was in what he'd accomplished, being questioned over spending and leadership was understandably hard for Barr, who'd grown up in a working-class home, lived much of his forties like someone just out of college, spent so much of his own time and money to get Green Dot going—and gotten so much good done in such a short time. "I drove us hard, but I left that organization with a pretty clear record of success," he said. Indeed, many still believed that Barr's accomplishments and skill were extraordinary. "What he's doing is more important than almost anything else going on in charters or in broader district reform," said Justin Cohen, president of the Mass Insight Education School Turnaround Group. "He gets things that other folks don't get, namely that real reform won't happen unless existing systems and power structures are disrupted, not just ignored." There wasn't much antipathy toward Barr on campus at Locke, either. "He built this place," said Coach Vic, the campus aide, waving his hands to show the leafy quad and the clean hallways. "He was the reason Bill Gates came to this school and gave us all that money."

20

TURNAROUND FEVER

Little did Petruzzi or anyone else know that the chance to do another turnaround would arrive so quickly that Green Dot might not be ready in time.

The unexpected opportunity resulted in large part from the efforts of a recently elected school board member named Yolie Flores. A social worker by trade, Flores was elected to the school board in 2007; she voted in favor of approving the conversion of Locke into a charter school operated by Green Dot. Two years later, she wanted desperately to do something bigger to fix Los Angeles schools than anyone else was talking about. "It was like there was a fire and no one was calling 911," she said. Flores tore a map showing just how few South Central students graduated high school with enough credits to go to a four-year college, wrote "UNACCEPTABLE" on it with a big red marker, and posted it on her door for everyone to see. Then, during the spring and summer of 2009, as Locke was finishing its first year under Green Dot, Flores gathered some like-minded school reform leaders together and devised a plan that would give district schools and teachers a chance—along with charters and other outside nonprofits—to make big changes. It was time for everyone to put up or shut up.

Eventually growing to include about three hundred schools, the plan was to let managers of charter schools, other nonprofits, and inventive district educators bid on public schools and, if approved, run them. Dubbed "Public School Choice" (PSC), the plan would eventually hand over roughly a third of the most vexed schools in the city and dozens of new facilities to teachers and outsiders who thought they could do better. In just the first year, sixty schools would be handed over from the school district—twelve of them among the lowest-performing schools in the district.

If passed, the plan would be an amazing, whirlwind change of direction. Three years before, the idea of allowing a single high school campus to operate under Green Dot had been an enormous, all-consuming policy decision. Now, delegating control over a single school seemed like a minor step.

In many ways Flores's plan—bringing in a mix of charters, hybrids, and teacher-led teams to revamp different schools—was as an outgrowth of Barr's original vision, the Locke turnaround effort on steroids. Barr had helped energize school reform advocates in Los Angeles and shown that district teachers wanted change just as much as parents and outsiders. According to NewSchools Venture Fund's CEO, Ted Mitchell, who would eventually become a Green Dot board member, the Flores initiative was a "direct descendent" of Barr's efforts.

Not everyone agreed that the origins went back to Green Dot. "There's no direct line between them," said Flores about the Green Dot connection. And no one seemed to think that Barr (or Green Dot) should take the lead in turning the proposal into reality. Having Barr at the front "worked for a while," said one insider who asked not to be named. "But now that we're not talking about one school anymore but rather talking about the entire school system, that requires people to play in the sandbox together."

However, one of the groups involved in the effort to win approval was called Parent Revolution, led by a former Green Dot deputy named Ben Austin. "Steve saw around the corner on at least two things," said Austin. "First was the idea of a 'reform' union contract. Second was Locke, which set the precedent for the really big macro changes we're pushing right now." In the run-up to the August school board decision, Public School Choice proponents like Austin rallied parents to make calls and appear at events showing their support, and kept close tabs on board members' shifting concerns—many of the same strategies Green Dot had used to win control over Locke two years before. They pushed hard and left no stone unturned, and the organizing savvy worked. The resolution passed the school board six to one.

There were a couple of key differences, however, between Green Dot's original idea and this massive new initiative. First was that there were now gleaming new facilities up for grabs, not just struggling, worn-out schools like Locke. Second was that no one from Green Dot was heading the effort. Petruzzi was focused on the second year of Locke and improving the performance of its other schools. Barr was working on starting his national effort, Green Dot America. He was ecstatic when the board approved the citywide initiative, but he stayed in the background. "You build these organizations, get really good people to lead them, but they can't succeed if you're always there," said Barr, sitting in an Adirondack chair in the garden of his home. "Ben's kicking ass. I don't need to be going to church groups every Sunday. I don't need to be marching all the time anymore." He joked that at least now the teachers union had Austin to hate instead of him. "Do I miss it?" he said, looking a little irritated at the question. "Of course."

For a time it seemed as though the plan was proceeding just fine on its own, but then in February the teachers union and its allies in organized labor rallied ferociously against "giving away" schools to outside organizations and pressured the school board to give most of the sixty schools available in the first year to educators and community groups, not charter operators, who only got four schools. Teachers wanted to run their own schools, but didn't necessarily want to go charter; reform advocates were outspent and outmaneuvered in the late stages of the game; and charter organizations didn't apply for as many schools as they could have—or for tougher "turnaround" schools. The *Los Angeles Times* blasted the charter networks, questioning their commitment to equity.

Behind the scenes, Petruzzi had considered having Green Dot apply to take over Jefferson High School, the place they'd come so close to getting five years before. But he'd already committed to opening two new middle schools for 2010–2011, and the economy was doing so poorly that he worried about a second turnaround pulling Green Dot under. (In fact, a similar charter school network would veer toward bankruptcy the following year, a fate that could easily befallen Green Dot.)

Had Barr still been in charge, it's hard to believe that the Flores initiative would have fallen apart at the end or that Green Dot wouldn't have applied to take over a second broken high school. Green Dot wasn't "ready" when it got Locke. It wasn't ready for much of its history. During the previous decade, Barr had amassed a tremendous amount of public credibility and possessed unmatched political skills. "The Steve Barr of two years ago would have been a powerful ally," said Mike Piscal, a longtime rival who at the time headed a charter network in South Central. But times had changed. Now it seemed as though charter advocates were as wary of Barr as they were of the district and the union. And now, because Barr was no longer head of Green Dot, they didn't have to work with him.

••

A couple of months after the reform effort fell apart in Los Angeles, Barr appeared on stage in front of a packed Washington DC hotel conference room. The topic was "political savvy." Should education reformers get involved in political campaigns, legislative fights, and policy issues as only a handful of organizations and individuals like Barr had done—or leave advocacy and politics to outside groups and focus on educating kids?

Barr sat hunched over in his chair, fiddling with a water bottle. The panelists sat in a bare row of chairs facing the audience, without the usual table and water carafe "You're in politics whether you like it or not," said Barr, whose face shone under the hot lights set up to capture the event on video. "Taking a kid and $8,000 dollars away from a school system is bare-knuckled politics."

This was vintage Barr—reminding everyone that reform was political, and that only by engaging in the politics of reform could reformers hope to make larger changes. And he wasn't alone in pushing the idea. "If you search your heart and feel uncomfortable with certain [political] tools . . . get over it," said another panelist, Jonah Edelman, cofounder of an advocacy organization called Stand for Children, which included political fundraising and direct lobbying in its efforts. "This really needs to be 'by any means necessary.'"

Yet among many school reform organizations there remained a deep and abiding distaste for this kind of work—a fear of politics, a concern about lobbying rules that apply to nonprofits, a lack of understanding about how politicians think and act, and a concern about the consequences of going to battle. Not everyone was convinced—not even all of those on the panel—that direct involvement was the way to go.

"Is it really in TFA's interest to jump in all of these fights? Probably not," said panelist Andrew Rotherham, cofounder of several Washington education think tanks. One of Barr's earliest proponents, Rotherham believed that education groups should make strategic decisions about whether to get involved directly or not. One of the most well-known reform organizations of the last twenty years, TFA, rarely involved itself in political disputes in the districts where it was active. Most important, according to Rotherham, reformers should avoid developing "a taste for blood."

"What you did with Green Dot was amazing," said Rotherham, addressing Barr directly. "But when you enter that fray you put a target on yourself."

Critics had been quick to jump on Locke's failure to increase student achievement dramatically in the first year, and on the financial and organizational changes that had taken place during the fall. Once considered necessary, "extreme" turnarounds like the one at Locke were now generating opposition and doubt. Increasingly portrayed as disruptive, unfair, and ineffective—as a way to blame teachers for districts' inaction, or as a distraction from deeper societal problems—turnaround efforts in places like Chicago, New York, and Central Falls, Rhode Island, were now being treated as a fool's errand, uncertain and likely to be ineffective, a speculative bubble, a fad. Wouldn't it be better—easier, faster, even, to do things that were less controversial: to start lots of new schools instead of fixing existing ones, for example, rather than firing teachers and trying to turn existing schools around; to work more cooperatively?

Mavericks like Barr were admired, to be sure, but by spring 2010 they also seemed vulnerable and extreme. The economy had fallen apart; the enthusiasm for Barack Obama had waned. Somewhere along the line, in part by his own doing and in part through larger dynamics unfolding around him, Barr had crossed the line from maverick to rogue. Indeed, it was unclear whether Barr was up there on stage as a model or as a cautionary tale.

21

DOING IT ALL OVER AGAIN

The first day of the second year under Green Dot, athletic director Stephen Minix was set to give a speech at a gala event held on the Paramount lot in Hollywood. Celebrity attendees included Alicia Keys, Salma Hayek, J. J. Abrams, Andre Agassi, and Arianna Huffington; comic Stephen Colbert was the host. "Hopefully I don't make an ass out of myself," wrote Minix a couple of days beforehand. His speech was a bit hokey, and he'd never spoken in front of an audience as big as this one was going to be. But he was otherwise well suited to his unofficial new job as the public face of the Locke turnaround effort, a role formerly played by Cubias.

Named as athletic director in the first year under Green Dot, the affable former athlete made visitors feel comfortable walking around the campus, then returned to his desk in the athletic department clubhouse and office and happily talked trash with the kids who hung out there playing table tennis. His hair was usually shaved down almost bald, his beard cropped close, with sparkly earrings shining from each ear and a big smile revealing startlingly white teeth. Raised in the Seattle-Tacoma suburbs, the biracial Minix was light-skinned enough that kids sometimes asked him "what he was." He'd arrived at Locke in 2002 fresh out of graduate school and became a fixture around the campus during the next six years. He was engaged to a former special education teacher at Locke. During one of the informal tours he sometimes gave, Minix met a VP for Viacom who said he wanted Minix to do some public speaking. Minix was happy to oblige.

Up on stage, Minix wore a tan suit and a light-blue dress shirt, flashed his Cheshire cat grin out at the crowd, and delivered his remarks with ease. Afterwards, he met Arianna Huffington, founder of the *Huffington Post*, and several other celebrities and bigwigs who offered him phone numbers and job opportunities.

The Viacom event was just the first of several media appearances that would feature Minix during Locke's second year under Green Dot. Later that fall, he appeared in a video segment commissioned by the U.S. Department of Education, as well as in another mini-documentary about the school produced by *GOOD* magazine. In January, he would be the only person from Locke invited to attend a big pay-per-view boxing match viewing party at Barr's home. A few weeks later, Minix would go to a private screening of *Waiting for "Superman,"* the school reform documentary produced by the same people who created *An Inconvenient Truth*. Minix would be the only one there from Locke.

"He's the golden boy for the Dot," said Coleman. "Absolutely."

••

Locke began its second year a few days after Labor Day weekend, and by all accounts the opening days of class went much more smoothly than they had the first year—and much more smoothly than they usually had in the past. Locke was as big or bigger than it had ever been—thirty-two hundred students overall. Kids weren't dropping out as much as in the past, or transferring to other schools. Their return was one of Locke's biggest successes and most serious challenges. But teachers had classrooms. Kids had schedules. There wasn't any of the confusion or faulty scheduling that had marred things last year. Hobbs Hall, the auditorium used as a holding tank for kids without schedules, was empty within days. Cubias even cut his long hair.

Easing the process was that they'd made some key changes over the summer: abandoning the burdensome tucked-in-shirt requirement (replaced by a ban on hoodies that weren't black, white, or grey) and eliminating bus routes that weren't being used. Perhaps the most noticeable change was the remodeled front entrance to the school. Where a swinging gate had stood in the past there was now a solid blue metal security door that funneled visitors toward a second door going into the Welcome Center, where a school clerk and a security guard were stationed permanently. The end effect was to make the front of the school look like something meant to prevent forcible entry (or a bomb blast).

"They got the same gates at the jail when I went to go see my uncle," said a student.

Security remained a big concern. Lt. Moore was moved to a back-office job, and the two school district police officers were replaced by a tall-booted deputy from the Los Angeles County Sheriff's Department. ("You do *not* fuck with the sheriffs," said the head of the Green Dot security operation.) Just a few days into the school year, the deputy stopped and searched two teenagers who were riding their bikes up and down in front of the school, peering over the gates trying to see past the black tarps. One had a gun concealed in his shoe; the other had a knife. "They wasn't here for nothing," said the head of the security guards. Then, gesturing out toward a quad full of kids having lunch and playing handball, he added, "What you see out there is a false sense of safety."

Big Locke would be spared much of the fighting and mischief that had hindered progress in the past. Formerly stuck at his post, Officer Byrd now floated around campus as a gang intervention specialist picking up tidbits of news about beefs and looming conflicts. The guards spent less and less time worried about kids on campus and were confident that they knew what was going on in the streets surrounding the school as well. "Last year, everyone looked wrong to us," said Moore's replacement in charge of the daily patrols. "This year we don't even have to get out of the car." Yet dangers remained. One of the school's students would be beaten badly near his home by a group of teens who wanted his car. Another would be shot after a weekend party over spring break.

Otherwise, much remained the same. The bell to start school and mark the beginnings and endings of classes still rung faintly. The classroom doors remained unmarked, most of them, except for room numbers, as did the hallway walls, except for the occasional hand-lettered spirit or event poster. Kids still sold junk food during breaks, only now they had larger bags of chips and regular deals with local bodegas for supplies. Café tables in the covered eating area replaced some of the blue metal picnic tables, making the area look a little less institutional. Big Locke now shared the main building with two of the baby Lockes, which were growing in size as the numbers of black shirts and white shirts were shrinking.

Most of the kids' faces were the same, too. Rhonda was back, as was Kerón and his buddy Anthony. Most of Moody's charges were back, as were Cubias's and Kaplowitz's "special project" kids. Even Johnny, the student who'd been shot and paralyzed the previous spring right before graduation, would return to Locke. Perhaps the biggest surprise was the return of Ricky, the sour, argumentative student whom Cubias had sent to Locke 4 last year. "My biggest mistake was to let that kid go to the green shirts," said Cubias. Locke 4 was supposed to be a good place for kids who didn't fare well in traditional classrooms, but the program was increasingly the subject of questions and concerns. Now Ricky was back in the black shirts, going to class and making decent grades. He still mouthed off to Cubias and Coach Vic and anyone else who'd listen—the kid just didn't have much good to say—but he was doing his work and avoiding the outright defiance that had gotten him in so much trouble the year before. In his office, Cubias showed off a printout of Ricky's PowerPoint presentation—an English assignment—about legalizing marijuana. "That's Ricky Cubias," said Cubias, tapping the printout with a long finger. "My son."

"Under the old Locke," said Coleman, "Ricky would have been a dropout."

After spending last year with three grade levels of students and as many as eight hundred students—far more than intended—Cubias's black shirts were down to just 525 juniors and seniors. Finally, they were the size they were supposed to be. For the black shirts, the new school year was shaping up to be much less hectic than the year before. Part of it was that the school was smaller, but a lot of it had to do with experience: the kids knew what to expect from the new Locke, and the teachers who had been new last year knew what to expect from the kids. Cubias, Moody, and Kaplowitz remained in charge of the school. Ronnie Coleman was there watching over the whole operation, ready to backstop them whenever necessary. (She still couldn't quite believe she'd survived the previous year. "How did I actually live through that?" she said. "I have no idea.")

"I hate to say it, but it's pretty much cush now," said Coach Vic, the campus aide who liked to sit at his post and read books while classes were in session. "All we do this year is take phones and iPods to Moody."

"I get teased sometimes that now I'm stealing," said Moody, the hard-working dean of students. "But I put in the work last year, and I'm still hollering in the hallways. I'm still the same guy. I'm still the big bad wolf. The only difference is that during class time I can get things done."

"It's not cush—but it's not the same," said Cubias. "I feel stress, but it's regular work stress, not that stuff that keeps you up at night."

Now a second-year administrator, Cubias was somewhat faster on his paperwork, and showed up at meetings he would have previously ignored. He continued to ride herd on kids who stepped out of line—a group that was becoming smaller and smaller. "All my snakes are little worms," said Cubias, referring to the troublemakers and knuckleheads who had spent so much time in his office last year.

Yet the stakes remained extremely high and the outcome uncertain. Would Cubias and other adults at the school be able to build on the successes of the whirlwind first year and make Locke substantially better academically? Could Green Dot transform itself from an overstretched start-up into a strong, healthy organization—capable of supporting all its schools and adding more?

"There's a whole lot riding on Locke," said Ben Austin, the former Green Dot staffer. "We're either going to show that Locke is on a trajectory for transformative change, or that Locke needs some refining."

••

The relative calm was shattered suddenly when, barely into the fourth week of school, head counselor Emily Kaplowitz stopped showing up for work. One day she was there. The next day she was gone. There was no warning series of events, nothing that happened that anyone could think of. Up to that point, Kaplowitz had been working doggedly as she had the year before, putting in long hours and showing up on weekends. She had worked so hard that she lost her voice during the first week of school.

At first it seemed to be a day-by-day thing. Then it was a week. Then two. Her first-floor office remained untouched. The college posters and banners and memorabilia from last year were still everywhere. What happened? No one knew. Kaplowitz wasn't answering phone calls or text messages. A few days into Kaplowitz's absence, Coleman had pulled the other counselors out of a meeting and told them that it wasn't clear if and when Kaplowitz was coming back. Coleman couldn't say what happened. Then she repeated much the same conversation with Cubias and Moody. They all scrambled to fill in as best they could. Kaplowitz was in charge of a large group of students and was one of few people on campus who knew how to get things done. She ran events, knew how to access files and data, and knew all the kids. She could change kids' schedules, get them services. It was a big hole to fill. There was a lot of work to be done.

At first, there was relatively little concern. Locke was still a big place. Teachers and staff took days off to deal with personal issues all the time. So it was a few weeks before everyone really took note that Kaplowitz hadn't come back to school. "I was in complete denial," said English teacher Maggie Bushek, who had worked closely with Kaplowitz. Then, in early November, Green Dot hired a new counselor to fill in for Kaplowitz. The new hire, a young woman whose dad had been one of the first graduates of Locke back in the early 1970s, was described as temporary.

Finally, in early December, two months after Kaplowitz stopped coming to school, the official announcement went out that she would not be coming back to Locke. But there was still no explanation for the sudden disappearance. Kaplowitz refused to tell anyone what happened. All that Green Dot would say was that she had "voluntarily resigned for personal reasons." Cubias wondered if he'd done enough to help Kaplowitz out if she needed it. "I feel a little bad," he said, sitting in his office. "I never reached out; I never tried to fight it." Coleman—one of the only people on campus who knew the whole story—felt similarly distraught, but also felt that there wasn't much she could have done to change the situation.

"People toss 'heartbreaking' around all the time," said Coleman, sitting behind her office desk. "But she was a friend—is a friend. She was trusted and valued here. That was the toughest thing I've ever done in my life." Although Coleman had fought for Cubias and the young teachers who'd had a drink at prom, the Kaplowitz situation was different. "I couldn't fight for her," said Coleman.

"Because of what she'd done?" I asked, having no idea what she'd done (and unsure I wanted to know).

Coleman's eyes flickered for a second, but then she nodded her head.

"Because of what she'd done."

The new counselor took down the University of Maryland banners and other personal items in the office and put them in a box. Cubias and the others filled in as best they could. Kaplowitz came to retrieve her belongings over the winter break, unseen by any of her former colleagues. Bushek tried to e-mail Kaplowitz but never got a response. "We never saw her again."

22

BECOMING A SCHOOL

It was a Wednesday morning, and the classroom was full of Locke teachers rather than students. At the front of the room stood two members of the math department demonstrating how to use something as simple as a folded-up construction paper booklet to help get kids sharing ideas and retaining information. Used properly, the booklets add visual stimulation to lessons and help engage students with tangible as well as conceptual activities—a way of mapping information physically as well as mentally (like flash cards, outlines, or dioramas).

This was the ninety-minute professional development session for teachers—the new incarnation of the weekly sessions that had been a bit of a mess last year when Coleman and Cubias filled them with announcements and reminders (so-called "administrivia") rather than ideas and materials that could help inexperienced teachers survive long enough to become more effective in the classroom. At one point Coleman had resorted to having them read *The 7 Habits of Highly Effective People*, which was inspiring but didn't offer much direct help for a drowning first-year teacher.

This year, Coleman had handed the weekly sessions over to two of Locke's best teachers. Their goal was not just to talk about what worked in the classroom but to demonstrate it as well—and to give teachers something concrete they could use right away. Some of the ideas they were presenting were simple: turning music on during a solo reading period, having the kids move from one part of room to another to break up a long class period. They demonstrated classroom management skills on members of the English department, some of whom tended to revert into goof-offs when not in front of their own students. Other elements they presented—balancing classroom structure against student engagement, preparing students to transition between activities—were more nuanced.

It was only now, in year two, that Locke really started to become a school. The crisis mentality was gone; the makeshift arrangements were less ubiquitous. The school still wasn't buttoned-down by any means, but there were lots of rules and schedules and systems that had been missing in the past—useful ones, by and large. There was a monthly tour of the school to accommodate the constant flow of visitors who wanted to see what was going on, and arrows on the floors showing tardy kids where to line up each morning. Cubias and Coleman and Boulden were doing all the things that they couldn't do last year—including, finally, putting classroom instruction on the front burner.

Last year a handful of teachers, just like some students, had fallen through the cracks, and most teachers had felt as though they were pretty much on their own. This year, teachers said they felt that they knew each other better and were able to keep an eye out for each other. By year's end Big Locke would lose just eleven teachers out of 115 who began the year, or roughly 90 percent. Even the worst teachers were in class teaching lessons with some sense of what they were supposed to be doing. "Our shittiest teacher is in there doing a lesson," said Cubias. "He might not be doing enough with it. But he's trying."

It wasn't just teachers who were getting more supervision and support. There were new services and programs for kids, too. Psychological services and social supports were coordinated to address students' emotional issues. A much-needed program for extremely low-level literacy instruction was being tried out. "We're leaving no stone unturned," said one of the Green Dot cluster leaders.

In the classrooms and hallways, teachers saw small but promising signs that they were getting through. Kids bringing their bikes to school showed that they felt campus was safe. Kids pulling out books and paper outside of class demonstrated that the stigma against doing work was decreasing.

For Cubias, the second year was reaffirming his sense that academic results flowed from relationships. "At the end of the day, the school's performance is going to be dependent on your treatment of the students," he said one day out on the handball courts, herding four wayward students back to the main building. "We show the kids that we want to make things better for them, and the kids show us that they believe us in doing that." The year was going phenomenally as far as Cubias could see, though of course there were regular hiccups. "Is it perfect? No. You *are* going to get cussed out by an angry student once in a while. That's just the way it is."

Cubias remained a fanatic for supervision, a tireless El Salvadoran shepherd wandering the halls and finding stray kids to bring back to class or to his office. Most staff bored of supervision; Cubias loved it more than pretty much anything else, he just loved being out there with the kids.

Attention to the basics of school culture hadn't disappeared. In some ways it had expanded. In addition to the massive new security gate at the front of the school, the halls were now lined with a gauntlet of teachers standing in their doorways welcoming students into class and greeting (or chiding) kids passing in the halls. Every day at dismissal time, Moody grabbed his radio and walked around the corner to 111th and Towne to supervise a corner that had a lot of foot traffic. Most days it was pretty quiet, though he did call for backup one day when a kid who'd been kicked out of another Green Dot school got angry at being told to leave the area. The security team swooped in within seconds. ("Now he knew," the security chief said with a small smile.) As of April there had been just one security lockdown (in response to shots fired a couple of streets over), and not a single pepper-spraying incident on campus. One-on-one fights were still relatively common, but combatants were now referred to school staff for suspension or a parent conference rather than to law enforcement.

The pressure to do better academically was stronger than ever. Teachers and administrators were spending a lot more time looking at how students were progressing in each teacher's classroom. Every few weeks there was a new set of graphs to look at—green indicated that a teacher's students were making strong progress and meeting the state academic standards. "That's what we're looking for," said Coleman, pointing to one teacher's printout. "Fields of green." Academic results were broken out by student, by class, by subject, and by teacher. The color-coded charts showed gaps and weaknesses in what was going on in the classroom, and provoked discussions about what teachers could be doing and what might not be working as well as they'd thought. Not everyone believed that the data were perfect, but there was much less talk about how difficult Locke kids were, now that it could be shown that some teachers were pulling things off.

"Last year was all about culture," said Cristina de Jesus, Green Dot's chief academic officer. "This year's all about instruction." Teaching quality was the stuff that was going to make or break the turnaround effort in the long run—along with beefing up the support services for kids whose problems were particularly acute and the mentality that graduating and going to a four-year college was normal. All the safety and civility in the world wouldn't mean anything—would eventually hollow out all that had been done so far—if Locke kids didn't finish high school, graduate, and stand a decent chance of doing college-level work at a real, four-year college. It wasn't enough for kids to be in class and pass their courses anymore. They had to learn something, too, and begin to see the benefits that came with getting past high school and pushing through to a college degree.

"These kids need to get up out of here," said Moody, prowling the halls for errant kids. "I'm not talking about no small-time school like Southwest Community College, either."

Toward that end, Green Dot was building and piloting something it had never had before—a clear instructional model. Academic recommendations, lesson planning, and common expectations were all being rolled out so that teachers knew what they were supposed to be doing and had some basic tools showing them how to be successful in the classroom. A model student handbook was finally created, including both districtwide policies and issues that schools could decide on their own (within the law). Attendance record keeping and policies were straightened out to a certain extent, too. "It's amazing what people can get done if they're provided with some basic tools," said de Jesus.

Ironically, the school looked worse even as it was working better. Once beautiful, parts of the quad were being torn up to create outdoor eating spaces—round white tables at the corners of the quad, each with fixed metal umbrellas. The quad was being turned into a food court, but for the moment it looked raw and dug up like a construction site. And a few things got harder rather than easier. Having retained so many kids who would have otherwise dropped out last year, this year's student body included more kids who hadn't fully bought into Green Dot's system and—hard as it seemed to believe—were even more deficient academically than the previous year's group. This year's seniors included lots of kids who'd been retained in previous years—boys especially. Integrating the special education program was another big challenge. Like other charter networks, Green Dot was determined to show that it could serve special education students, but there had been a year's lag in getting its program in place.

One of the most obvious remaining flaws was Locke 4, the green shirts, the small alternative program that was supposed to help kids catch up on credits but didn't seem to be doing very well at its job. Kids who were sent there were clamoring to get back into the black shirts or dropping out, rather than getting caught up on their credits. Sending kids over to the green shirts wasn't a solution, yet despite more than a year's frustrating experiences, administrators had gotten into the habit. "They turned it into a reform school," said Coach Vic. "If you even act funny, you go to green shirts." But the program hadn't changed much since last year. Security guards spent a lot of their time responding to calls from there. "They only stay there a short time," admitted Cubias, referring to kids who were sent to Locke 4. "You're pretty much on your own over there." But he still saw some value in the program in that it kept kids who would otherwise have dropped out connected to school. Being at school regularly would lead to passing classes, Cubias believed. "You take a kid from 10 to 20 percent attendance to 70 to 80 percent and that will lead to academics eventually."

Coleman remained convinced about the overall progress, though she understood it was sometimes harder to see than it had been last year. "I think it's easy for people to lose sight of the wins," she said. "The easier life gets, the more we bitch about more and more minor things." Sometimes she tagged along on the monthly visitor tours in order to get a reminder of how things had been and how good they were now.

Fixing Locke, like most good things in life, was a labor of love. It wasn't happening overnight, but it was happening. Green Dot wasn't going anywhere; that message was finally sinking in. Now the educators at Locke just needed more time to keep things on the upswing before time and patience (and money) ran out.

23

FIRING EVERYONE

It was Wednesday, March 10, 2010, a couple of weeks before spring break, a training day without any kids on campus. The dress was casual—teachers were wearing shorts and flip-flops they would otherwise never wear while teaching.

Things weren't so relaxed in Coleman's first-floor office, however. All day long, the principal sat there firing some of her favorite teachers. One by one, they came into the sunny room. Most had no clue what was about to happen, never imagining that they might not be able to come back to finish out the third and final year of Big Locke. With Green Dot's head of human resources sitting next to her, Coleman told each teacher what was going on. The school would be drastically smaller next year. Who stayed was based on what courses kids needed and a ranking system set up with the union, based on years of experience, certification, and classroom evaluations. It wasn't anything personal. Did they have any questions? She felt horrible about what she was doing, but there were a lot of people to go through, so she didn't have much time to spare before moving on to the next person. But there was little relief. Big Locke's faculty was going down from sixty-two teachers to twenty-three. Two teachers were being let go for every one who got to stay.

Taken by surprise, English teacher Maggie Bushek broke down in tears when she found out she had to find another job. Bushek had voluntarily taken the lowest-level readers in the school into her classroom, and picked up a slew of reading intervention techniques to reach them. She'd taken over the school newspaper and launched a Web site. She'd worked her heart out. Math teacher Stephanie Avila, by many accounts one of the very best teachers in the school, was also left out; her paperwork wasn't in order. Some of Locke's best people were being told that they couldn't stay at Big Locke or—for those whose certifications weren't completed—at *any* Green Dot school.

Technically, no one was being fired. They were being "displaced." And the changes weren't taking effect immediately. Their jobs were safe until the end of the school year, and they were being promised consideration at other Green Dot schools on campus next year. But to those sitting across from Coleman that morning, it sure felt like being fired.

Then, in the middle of it all, Coleman received a text message from her domestic partner, Reta, a PE teacher in nearby Long Beach, who'd just gotten a layoff notice that morning. "I'm sitting here telling people that they're not going to come back next year, and then it hits me at home," said Coleman.

••

Coleman had done her best to make sure there were no surprises. Everyone knew that Big Locke would shrink every year. Seniors graduated, and the baby Lockes took the incoming freshmen. She'd explained the ranking system that had been developed by the home office and the union; years of experience were part of the formula, along with classroom evaluations like those she and Cubias did every year. But not everyone had paid attention or taken action to get their certification in order. And even then, it wasn't clear until the last moment exactly how many teachers would be needed next year for each subject, who was going to graduate school or moving to another part of the country. There were a lot of moving pieces. As a result, there were some unexpected results when it came to who was staying and who had to find somewhere else to go. Some teachers with experience and credentials would have to leave, while others with less experience and degrees could stay.

"They said it was about her evaluations," said one of Bushek's English department colleagues. "We all kind of think it's kind of shady."

"I guess I—I didn't make the cut," said a second-year Spanish teacher, still stumbling a little bit over her response.

Coleman understood the reactions. The teachers who'd voted for Green Dot two years before felt a lot of ownership of the turnaround effort. "They want to stay and finish this out. But then others who were last-minute hires get to stay. People are like, 'How did *that* work?'"

Part of the surprise came from the fact that there hadn't been anything nearly as dramatic by way of downsizing at the end of the previous year, when Big Locke had gone from three grade levels down to two. Unexpected funding from the state, plus the need for lots of students to take courses they had failed, meant that fewer than a dozen teachers had to leave between the first and second years. This year, the bloodbath wasn't a rumor. The reality was that Big Locke, once sixteen hundred students strong, was going down to just one grade level next year—one last crop of seniors—and then disappearing completely after that. It was just an issue of how many of each kind of teacher were going to be needed. Each year, there were fewer kids—and fewer teaching jobs. This was the hidden heartbreak built into Green Dot's phase-out, phase-in transformation model. All the students who had already been attending Locke got to continue at the school and graduate out with a core of familiar faces at the front of the classroom; their path was fundamentally unchanged. But only a few of the teachers who were at old Locke before were going to get to stay and see the last of the old Locke kids through to graduation.

Teacher evaluations played a big role, too—and didn't always favor teachers kids liked or who seemed the most at ease in class. "Sometimes it's not your stellar teacher who's getting good results," said Coleman, who had access to data comparing how much teachers moved kids' scores, though those data were not a formal part of the process. She described one teacher whose classroom work wasn't anything flashy but who had an amazing ability to help struggling kids pass the state exit exam. "He does a straight-up job and uses his time really well," she said. "I gave him a ton more of those kids for the next time around."

Another little-noted factor was that teacher certification was given the most heft in the ranking system Green Dot was using. Certification is the bureaucratic process through which teachers are approved to teach. Teachers are supposed to be certified in the subject area in which they are assigned, meaning that they have passed tests established for their subject by the state. Districts and schools are supposed to avoid putting disproportionate numbers of unqualified or out-of-field teachers in front of students. But few of those in education circles give certification much weight—teachers' classroom practice, education background, and other factors are considered much more important. (Many private schools don't even bother with certification, and most charters pay as little attention to it as they have to.) Green Dot was making certification a priority. Why? The district "threatened to not renew our charters if we weren't 100 percent NCLB compliant," said Petruzzi, "even if they are not [100 percent compliant] either."

And so, more than two years after the school had been legally freed from the school district, and twenty months since Green Dot had taken over the campus, Locke remained closely tied to the outside web of bureaucracy. In some regards these connections seemed positive: Locke still had to be accredited by a regional accrediting agency; it still had to have a special education administrator on campus to ensure that kids received the services they required; its records were audited by the board; its students had to pass the state exit exam in order to graduate. But in this particular realm of teacher certification, the bureaucratic ties didn't seem to favor kids' education. Teachers who weren't certified couldn't stay at Locke or get hired at another Green Dot school no matter how good they were with the kids or how much impact they had on student achievement. A teacher who was better in the classroom would lose out to a counterpart who was fully qualified on paper.

To see certification playing such a big role at Locke was hard to watch. Teachers scrambled to get their paperwork in or (as in several teachers' cases) corrected. Administrators made layoff decisions based on bureaucratic qualifications that had little to do with quality. Green Dot claimed it couldn't afford to do anything else; the district would revoke its charter or deny new ones if it didn't comply. But the answer wasn't entirely satisfying. What's the point of being a charter school if you have to follow all the district's rules anyway? And if a charter school's results were strong, then shouldn't its hiring and firing decisions be left alone? Green Dot didn't seem willing to risk challenging the district's edicts.

••

A few weeks later, on the first day back from spring break, Cubias showed up in the breezeway with his head shaved completely bald—the result of a lost bet on a soccer game, he claimed.

"He gets bored easily," said Coleman.

"Yeah, I was bored," admitted Cubias.

Coleman was feeling better about the downsizing now that the initial shock had passed. Green Dot was pretty much guaranteeing displaced teachers jobs within the Green Dot empire. A few key teachers had gotten their paperwork cleared up and would be allowed to stay, and several of the teachers who were being let go had already found jobs at other Green Dot schools or made plans to go somewhere else. There were a few uncertainties—what would happen to Mike Moody, for example—but not the collective unease that had followed the initial displacement announcement.

Once again, however, Coleman and Cubias were faced with unforeseen events. Over the two-week break, word had come down from the Dot that one of the principals at the baby Lockes was leaving immediately—pushed out or leaving voluntarily, no one really knew—and that Charles Boulden, Cubias's counterpart on the white side, was being tapped as the interim replacement. Boulden would be leaving nearly immediately, and Cubias and Coleman would have to fill in for him for the rest of the year. For Boulden it was a big pat on the back—a sign that Green Dot appreciated his work and was going to find a long-term place for him. For Cubias, being passed over for a promotion forced him to give his future with Green Dot a hard look. He tried to consider Boulden's departure as a kind of promotion for himself. Now he would be in charge of evaluating people throughout Big Locke, not just on the black side. But he wondered why Boulden had been given the job instead of him.

"Truth be told, I don't know if I would have said no," he said, leaning back in his office chair, long fingers clasped behind his head. There was no more talk about going back to the classroom, a move he'd thought about making in the past. "I was never really a math teacher," said Cubias. "I was just using math to do what I wanted to do." In front of him sat the hundred-page composition book he'd first started using halfway through his first year. The dappled black-and-white cover was marred with his doodles and smears, the bright yellow sticker slapped sideways across the front of it faded and smudged.

Even after more than a year and a half as an assistant principal, Cubias was still uncertain about his place. When it came to active supervision and school uniforms, he was unparalleled. He was improving on his paperwork, too, though he was the first to admit that others—his office manager, Maria, for example—picked up a lot of slack where he was still weak. Almost a full year after last spring's prom debacle, he thought he had a better relationship with the home office. "There's always going to be differences, but I've embraced and come to respect them and what they do, and they've come to respect what I do," he said. "They have come to value me as part of their organization. I kind of want to be a part of them." But Cubias lagged behind Boulden in several other ways. Even now, it sometimes seemed as though he couldn't be counted on for anything that involved a substantial amount of planning or preparation, no matter how small. He was easily distracted by immediate problems and failed to focus on long-term challenges. He rarely did things ahead of time. And—perhaps most important—he didn't convey respect or attentiveness to supervisors other than Coleman.

Still, Cubias seemed to have turned some sort of a corner professionally. Formerly reluctant to the point of rebellious when it came to attending meetings, he now appreciated the monthly training sessions for principals. He also liked hearing what Green Dot was all about directly from people at Green Dot rather than through the grapevine. "A lot of stuff kind of gets lost between Green Dot and us," he said. "It's good to know what they really say." He wasn't quite a worm, but he wasn't entirely a snake anymore, either. "It seems like he's really learned from the feedback he's been given and is thinking in terms of the Green Dot team instead of 'the Man' coming in to take over Locke," said de Jesus, who felt Cubias had been growing as an administrator and responding to coaching. "It takes time to gain trust in a new organization, especially given Locke's past," she said. "I can understand the process he's been going through." Cubias could be promoted to principal "depending on his readiness," said another Green Dot administrator.

Just a day or so later, Cubias got word from a student stopping by his office that the kids had voted him "most spirited" for this year's yearbook.

24

ALWAYS A SAINT

A round-faced senior named Lanelle wasn't wearing a black collared shirt, and also had on open-toed slippers that were prohibited by the school dress code.

"Call your grandma," said Cubias.

"I gotta be chill," said Lanelle, who was sporting big metal hoops in her ears and a small one going through one eyebrow. But then she smiled and called on her cell phone. A few minutes later, Lanelle's grandmother—whom she called "grandmamá"—walked up to the school carrying an oversized handbag.

"Why'd you get out of the car?" said Lanelle, arms spread wide. "I'm going home."

"For something as minor as that?" asked her grandmother. "Why can't they write you up or something?"

"This is not no job," said Lanelle.

"They can still write you up," came the response. "You just going to sit at home—that don't make sense."

"Tell my assistant principal," said Lanelle, nodding toward Cubias.

Grandmamá passed Cubias by and went straight to Principal Coleman's office.

"They sending her home because the dummy forgot her collared shirt," said Lanelle's grandmother. "How come they can't just write her up and take something away from her?"

"This is year two," said Coleman, ever patient. "She's a senior. She knows. She could stay here, but she can't go to class."

"That's dumb," said Lanelle, clearly displeased at the idea of spending the day at school but away from her friends. "Not even lunch?"

"You need to be punished," said her grandmother. "You need to suffer."

"Lunch with the principal—the kids hate it," said Coleman. Then, turning to Lanelle, she asked, "How are your grades, my dear?" Lanelle gave a weak smile in response.

"Lanelle generally does well with us," said Coleman to her grandmother. "She's a pistol. I fell in love with her last year."

"See, I'm a good kid," said Lanelle, eager to change the subject from her grades.

"I didn't say anything about good," said Coleman, smiling broadly.

Lanelle wasn't an angel, it was true. A straight-A student during her early elementary grades, she lost her mom at the end of junior high and started getting into fights often enough that she was sent to juvenile detention during her freshman year. Sophomore year wasn't much better. "I was really bad," she said. "I just got dropped off at school and never went to class." She got straight Fs. When Green Dot came along, she didn't immediately take to all the rules and regulations, either, but she got a lot of attention from administrators and teachers—who all said she was bright and capable if she could only manage her temper and complete some class work. Eventually she joined the group of kids who went to church and had breakfast with Moody most Sundays. Now she was sitting in class next to some of the people she used to beat up. She obviously still struggled to come to school in uniform and to get to class and stay there, and still relapsed frequently enough that it was uncertain whether she would catch up with her classmates. But it seemed as though she had a shot at participating in the graduation ceremony as long as she didn't mess up these last few weeks and undo all of her and everyone's else's hard work.

Each teacher and administrator at Locke could name a handful of kids who had been affected this way—kids who'd started out with serious challenges and somehow turned things around. Sometimes it was behavior issues. Sometimes it was problems outside the school. Other times it was "just" schoolwork. Too often, these kids made improvements, only to relapse in some way. There was always the risk of a last-minute collapse or an inexplicable return to bad old ways. It was now about a month before graduation—Green Dot's second year in charge of Locke—and Coleman, Cubias, and everyone else were holding on as best they could to make it until the end. The end-of-year exhaustion normal at any school seemed doubled, as though it had accumulated over two years and then been boosted with the question-riddled end-of-year downsizing and the generalized economic uncertainties. "I need a break," said the office manager. "I need to get out of the country." They were so much better at their jobs than they had been last year—and so much more tired.

••

The morning of graduation day itself, things seemed to be falling apart. Coleman was dismayed to find out that nobody from Green Dot had showed up at the weekend's alumni event on campus, missing an easy opportunity to mend fences with community members who remained suspicious of Green Dot's intentions. "They whiffed," said Minix, who'd attended the event. "All they had to do was show up and eat some food and smile." Then Coleman found that no one on campus had a copy of "Pomp and Circumstance" (or "Pompandstance," as someone described it on the radio), setting off a scramble to find or download a version. Meanwhile, a nearly constant stream of kids and teachers and parents came into Coleman's office to discuss last-minute crises and conflicts, of which there was no shortage. One of everyone's favorite kids, Rhonda, was being kicked out for getting caught stealing prom tickets from a teacher's desk; Cubias and Coleman were busy trying to get her enrolled at another Green Dot school for next year. The previous Friday, it had been revealed that at least ten Locke students had used a stolen password to give themselves credit for online courses they hadn't taken. It was a serious issue, and Coleman worried about how widespread it might be. (Boulden and Cubias took a more irreverent view: "They're not thinking about how to sneak into the dance anymore," quipped Boulden. "We're onto that white school shit now," said Cubias.) Perhaps most difficult of all, Coleman had to meet with the parents of two popular seniors who'd been told they couldn't participate in graduation after they had gotten into a dispute with security guards at Six Flags amusement park on grad night. "What a bitch I am, taking graduation away," said Coleman. A handful of other kids were already gone. Kerón and Anthony had long since stopped going to Locke. They had packed and left for a nearby junior college a few days before. They were supposed to get the last of the high school credits they needed there. One of Bushek's favorite kids, Jeremy, had been kicked out for being out of uniform one too many times.

Coleman handled most of this on her own. Cubias had gone home to make himself pretty, returning later in a spiffy light grey suit with slick white boots and a broad white belt. Then, just after lunchtime, police locked down the campus and a dark blue police helicopter began flying in tight circles over the streets next to the school, blowing up a lot of dust and making it hard for anyone to hold a conversation while it searched for a car thief on the run. "Are we really on lockdown?" asked one of the teachers. "That is *not* festive." But then finally the helicopter went away—the thief or thieves apprehended after a short chase—and the sun broke through, and things went forward as they usually did at Locke. The street vendors gathered to sell flowers and balloons to families arriving at the school. Coleman put on her gown—ironed this time in the counselors' office a few minutes beforehand—and walked over to the gym to get things organized for the arrival of the seniors, teachers, and families. Her mom was in town to see it all happen. Cubias's mom would be there, too.

The graduation ceremony itself was a much smaller affair than the previous year, when Barr had been the keynote speaker and the school had been on the front page of the newspaper. Neither Petruzzi nor Barr nor any elected officials attended—Barr went to the graduation at another Green Dot school instead—and there was no national press as there had been last year. "We're not big news anymore," said Coleman. Still, it was a sunny, calm day. On the field were 360 seniors sitting in light-blue gowns and hats, 247 of whom were eligible to get their diplomas. Lanelle was one of those who was there. She was eligible to participate in the graduation ceremony even though she would still have to come back for summer school to finish up her credits. "I'm the first girl in my family who's going to graduate," she said. The stands were full of parents and cousins and friends. And there were a lot of other things to celebrate. Locke wasn't just safe and orderly: it was a school. "Now kids know that there's life after Locke," said Ms. Burnett, the longtime clerk at the school. Burnett was going to be coming back, one of the last two of the clerks at Big Locke. Art and drama teacher Monica Mayall was coming back, too, in large part because she felt so good about the kids turning the corner and buying into classroom culture. By the end of the year, kids were ragging on each other about their GPAs and class rank rather than about clothes or music. "All right, Mr. Number 468," one kid would crack at another. Officially, they'd been building a college-going culture for the past two years, but more realistically they'd been building a safe environment and a class-going culture. Being ready for college would have to come later. "We have to win they *minds*," said Boulden.

Winning minds might sound easy but it was in reality harder than making the school safe, harder than finding dedicated teachers, harder in some ways than raising test scores. It wasn't just that Locke kids didn't go to college in great numbers, or do well once they got there; they didn't know how to learn, and they didn't believe that they could. Most of them didn't know anyone who had made it out of Watts, and considered those few who made it an exception or a fluke, like someone winning the lottery. In contemplative moments, Locke teachers admitted that the challenges ahead of them were just as big as the ones behind them. Indeed, a team of teachers visiting from Sacramento High School, now several years into its turnaround, had warned them that getting kids to believe that they can go to a good college was inordinately harder than making campus safe—and that there was a relatively narrow window of time during which the kids, the community, and the staff were open to a drastic change in beliefs. "Positive academic outcome expectations begin to rise quickly," warned the former Sac High principal.

••

Graduation was proceeding according to schedule when Cubias surprised nearly everyone by announcing from the podium that he wanted to introduce someone special. Wearing a dark striped suit with a crew-neck shirt underneath, Reggie Andrews, the former music teacher, strode up onto the stage from the place he'd been standing unnoticed since the beginning of the ceremony. Andrews and Cubias had stayed in loose touch over the past couple of years, and Cubias had arranged for a plaque to give to Andrews thanking him on behalf of the Locke community, news of which was included on the back of the program. The two men shook hands and hugged, then Andrews stepped toward the microphone.

There were a few uncomfortable looks shared onstage behind him and among a few of those in the crowd. No one had said anything about Andrews speaking to the students. He'd left on bad terms and didn't have much good to say about Green Dot's handling of the Locke turnaround. Standing there at the microphone in front of the graduating seniors, however, Andrews didn't vent his anger at what had happened to him personally. He talked to the students about having helped Green Dot come to Locke, for them. "I stood by my community," he said. He told the seniors that this was their day, and that there was genius in all of them, a sentiment not unlike the one in Barr's graduation speech the year before. He ended his remarks with the usual call and response: "Once a Saint," said Andrews. "Always a Saint," came the response from the students. Cubias hugged him again after the speech, and then Andrews walked down off the stage.

"Did you see that shit?" said Minix, standing over to the side, smiling and shaking his head at having Andrews speak. "For a second there I thought, 'Oh, no, we're about to burn.'"

"I knew I was taking a risk," said Cubias. "But I knew he's got class."

And then the ceremony wound down. The breeze started picking up, and the clouds came in and hid the sun. Flags snapped in the wind. Loudspeakers swayed gently against their ropes. Balloons swung and jumped. Coleman tried for a moment to stop guests from taking the flower arrangements from the field, but then let it go; the stage was stripped in seconds.

The day after graduation, Coleman led the last meeting of the year with staff. "This project changed me," she said. "I hope it changed you. We all came here to make things different for the kids. But most of us ended up being changed, too. It's been an amazing ride. We've pretty much done what we set out to do. We worked our asses off."

Cubias added a special thanks to the Locke teachers who had been open to Green Dot and had stayed on to help make the change. "You were the first people to convince me that this Green Dot thing would work. Thank you."

"Look at how many people who stood up to the district," said Coleman. "They didn't know what the change was going to be. They insisted on change, and then they dealt with the change that happened. Thank you for making this happen."

EPILOGUE

Things were *always* changing at Locke. A couple of nights before graduation, one of the baby Lockes held its year-end awards ceremony in Hobbs Hall, right next to the cafeteria. A roomful of freshmen and sophomores and their families filled the room, clapping and hollering as their principal, Rachelle Alexander, stood in front of the stage and praised kids for their academic accomplishments during the year. This was the face of the "new" new Locke. In the fall, Alexander's school would add a third grade level, while Big Locke would shrink down to just one grade level—the senior class—and a single hallway in the main building. A year after that, the last students from old Locke would be gone, and the five baby Lockes would take over the entire campus, serving kids from ninth through twelfth grades.

In the meantime, news came out that Big Locke's scores were up again—even more than the first year. The proficiency rates were still woefully low—in English, only 15 percent of Locke students met the state academic standards; and in math, only 7 percent. Raising scores would require "the patience to support teachers and schools through years of sustained, concentrated effort," noted the *Los Angeles Times*. An article in the *New York*

Times noted Green Dot had been given an extra $15 million by outside funders, of which $700,000 a year was being spent on security. Green Dot claimed the extra money was needed only because California's basic support for public education was so low.

But these results were much better than they had been, and Locke had increased the number of students who were proficient by 74 percent in English and by 295 percent in math over the past two years—in large part by retaining and testing seven hundred more students than had been previously included when the school was under the district's control. Big Locke's rating went up moderately from 540 to 582. Sixty-two percent of the kids who took the AP calculus test passed—a Locke record. Even more important, teachers continued to see signs of growth and promise: parents showing up to see if they could register their children; kids pulling books out of their backpacks and reading on their own when they had a little extra time in class. These were, according to one veteran teacher, "the first blooms of new flowers sprouting from what seemed as dead branches."

About halfway into the summer, Green Dot asked Cubias to take over Locke 4, the green shirts. The move gave Cubias the approval he so desired, an exciting new challenge, and a job that lasted past June 2011—and gave the students who were sent to Locke 4 a new chance. Locke 4 was filled with the most troubled kids, a mix of those who were severely behind in terms of credits, faring poorly in the regular Locke classroom, or back from juvenile detention, and it was perhaps the least successful program of any of the Locke schools. Coleman was sad to see Cubias leave her, but happy that now he would have his own school to run. "He's at his best right now—decisive, moving, building relationships. I love seeing him like this," she said, just before the third year started. Most of the other Locke veterans who'd helped at the beginning had also found decent places to land. Former principal Frank Wells was running a small alternative high school in Northern California. Music teacher Andrews retired with thirty-eight years in the system and lifetime benefits (assuming the state didn't go bankrupt). English teacher Bruce Smith was consulting here and there and hoping to start his own school. Though helping bring Green Dot to Locke hadn't benefited him individually, Smith remained extremely proud of what he'd done.

Although Green Dot was just a small part of *Waiting for "Superman,"* the documentary's September release generated renewed attention for Green Dot and for Barr—not so much for the Locke turnaround itself but for the need to fix broken schools and for Barr's idea of a new, different kind of union contract. During a period of no more than a couple of weeks in the early fall, Green Dot and Barr were mentioned in several articles and commentaries following the movie's release, including two *New York Times* opinion pieces. The success of Green Dot's unionized charter school network was an important touchstone. "The Green Dot contract helped all of us—not just charters—think about thinner and different contracts," said NewSchools Venture Fund's Ted Mitchell, a supporter who was now on the Green Dot board of directors.

Buoyed by the publicity, Barr was once again back in the fray. It was a critical time for Democratic reformers, many of whom were still deeply divided about charters and unions. Once again, he would try to show that unions weren't the enemy of school reform and that charters weren't the solution. He was eager to spread the word that there was an alternative to the traditional labor contract and the nonunion charter model—some sort of "new" unionism that would engage frustrated teachers young and old and help them push for changes that were being blocked by union locals dominated by older, more traditional teachers. "Seventy five percent of teachers out there don't get what the fuck their union is all about," said Barr. Maybe he could create momentum for a national reform movement of teachers, convincing some among them to run for school rep or to become a delegate or local president rather than giving up and leaving to start a charter. In the meantime, he sent his eldest daughter off to her first days of kindergarten at the local public elementary school.

Early in the fall, Petruzzi traveled to Washington to give Obama education officials his take on how best to revamp hundreds of schools around the country under the new $3.5 billion turnaround program. From Petruzzi's perspective, the Obama administration's initiative had the same fatal flaw that was in its predecessor, No Child Left Behind: it gave districts the option to do something vague and moderate with even their most failing schools—a "light" option that experience suggested would be the choice of many if not most. It provided a windfall of up to $6 million to failing schools without any requirement that they consider working with outside operators like Green Dot. Nationally, only thirty-one of 733 turnarounds would follow the Green Dot model in 2010–2011.

Back in Los Angeles, Petruzzi continued to preach that the real solutions to broken schools weren't in policies or program models or "prophets" but rather in extremely hard work and closely aligned efforts. Green Dot celebrated its tenth year in operation and reorganized its board to bring in a slew of new faces. Kept afloat thanks to Petruzzi's careful stewardship, Green Dot avoided the financial meltdowns that were crippling other charter networks, and was positioned to do another turnaround in the near future. Petruzzi was thinking that maybe the time would be right in September 2011, when Coleman and her team would be done with the last of the "old" Locke kids.

That would be fine with Coleman, who hoped she'd be asked to play a role. "I swore I wouldn't do it again, but I couldn't resist having the chance to do it right this time."

In September, Locke opened for its third year under Green Dot, focused on showing once again that, with tremendously hard work and sacrifice, a once-broken school could be improved in meaningful (if incomplete) ways. Coleman and her colleagues would have to reestablish the culture and form new relationships with all the new arrivals on campus. The baby Lockes would have to deal with being 50 percent bigger than they'd been the year before. In the meantime, Bushek got married. Moody got a job at one of the baby Lockes. Mayall finally resigned as union rep. Lanelle didn't finish up her credits right away, but planned to come back the second semester. Ricky, now a senior, was coming to school, but still struggling. There would be interruptions and surprises, sure. But everyone would keep pushing forward and, if past experience was any guide, would continue to make strides forward. They might never be able to keep the stray dogs out of the quad, but it might not really matter.

"We're not going anywhere," said principal Alexander, whose baby Locke now included three grade levels. "Give us time as long as we're showing progress. In the meantime, let's begin to focus on the positive stuff."

Selected Sources

Everything described in this book came from direct observation, interviews with eye witness observers, and written sources such as those listed here. In addition, I shared drafts of chapters with sources and witnesses and made corrections and additions where needed. In cases where accounts differed or no definitive information was available, I indicated the existence of a dispute and described both sides of the issues involved. Last but not least, the manuscript was independently fact-checked, and again changes were made.

Chapter 1: Desperate School Reform Superstar

Bain & Company report on Green Dot, 2004.

Jean Merl and Joel Rubin, "Troubled L.A. Campus May Be Taken Over," *Los Angeles Times*, August 11, 2005.

"Concerns over proposed Jefferson High Takeover," *Los Angeles Times*, August 21, 2005.

Jean Merl and Joel Rubin, "Marchers Urge Remaking L.A. Campus into Charters," *Los Angeles Times*, November 16, 2005.

Joel Rubin, "Effort to Take Over Campus Is Dropped," *Los Angeles Times*, December 7, 2005.

Judith Lewis, "The Secret of His Success," *Los Angeles Weekly*, December 7, 2006.

Los Angeles Times Most Influential List, 2006.

Joel Rubin, "A for Ambition," *Los Angeles Times*, February 20, 2007.

Sandra Tsing Loh, "Million Parent March, Part One: Spray On Some Bill Gates," KPCC, April 28, 2008.

Chapter 2: Getting Locke

"Locke Principal Rips L.A. Unified," *Los Angeles Times*, May 4, 2007.

Sam Dillon, "Maverick Leads Charge for Charter Schools," *New York Times*, June 24, 2007.

Stacey Childress and Christopher Kim, "Green Dot Public Schools: To Collaborate or Compete?" Harvard Business School, August 1, 2007.

Joel Rubin and Howard Blume, "Green Dot Charter Organization to Take Over Locke High School," *Los Angeles Times*, September 12, 2007.

Chapter 3: Year In Limbo

Jesse Katz, "The Test of Their Lives," *Los Angeles Magazine*, May 2007.

Peter C. Beller, "Watts Riot," *Forbes*, July 30, 2007.

Donna Foote, "Lessons from Locke," *Newsweek*, August 11, 2008.

ETS school violence report, *School Crime and Safety 2008*.

Donna Foote, *Relentless Pursuit: A Year in the Trenches with Teach For America* (New York: Knopf, 2008).

Michael McElveen, "Green Dot: Proponent of Educational Reform," *Huffington Post*, October 1, 2009.

Chapter 4: Unlikely Leader

"The Untidy Revolution," *Economist*, November 8, 2007.

Steve Lopez, "Watts' Locke High School Is Getting Whipped into Shape," *Los Angeles Times*, July 23, 2008.

Chapter 5: Scrambling for Teachers

Joe Williams, "Revolution from the Faculty Lounge," *PDK*, November 2007.

Chapter 6: The Gate

Howard Blume, "Rival Latinos and Blacks Start Melee on South L.A. Campus," *Los Angeles Times*, May 10, 2008.

Chapter 7: "New" Locke

"Los Angeles' Most Troubled High School Undergoes Transformation," *Nightline*, August 13, 2009.

Chapter 8: Stray Dogs in the Quad

"How Many Billionaires Does It Take to Fix a School System?" *New York Times Magazine*, March 9, 2008.

Chapter 9: In the Classroom

"Inside Locke High," SoCal Connected, KCET, December 4, 2008.

Alexander Russo, "Charters and Unions," *Harvard Education Letter*, January 2010.

Chapter 11: Mayall's Revenge

Green Dot–AMU contract, final version, 2007–2008.

Chapter 12: Rogue Cops

Nilaja Sun, *No child . . .* [play], 2006.

Chapter 16: The *New Yorker*

Stacey Childress and Christopher Kim, "Green Dot Public Schools: To Collaborate or Compete?" Harvard Business School, August 1, 2007.

Claudio Sanchez, "Green Dot's Takeover of L.A. Schools Gets Results," *All Things Considered*, NPR, December 17, 2007.

Alexander Russo, "The 'Neighborhood' Charter," *Huffington Post*, May 7, 2009.

Douglas McGray, "The Instigator," *New Yorker*, May 11, 2009.

"Promises to Keep," *Fox News*, Los Angeles, May 2009.

Sam Dillon, "As Charter Schools Unionize, Many Debate Effect," *New York Times*, July 27, 2009.

Chapter 17: "We Did It, Y'All"

"Building on What Works at Charter Schools," Committee on Education and Labor, June 4, 2009.

"Much Done, Much to Do at the L.A. Charter School," *Los Angeles Times*, June 25, 2009.

Chapter 18: The New Face of Green Dot

Five-year plan presented and approved by board, March 2009.

Green Dot press release, August 2009.

Barr resignation letter e-mail, October 28, 2009.

Chapter 19: Barr Steps Down

Kenneth Libby, "How'd Steve Barr Spend $50,866?" *Schools Matter*, October 30, 2009.

Adolfo Guzman Lopez, "Green Dot Public Schools Chairman Steve Barr Steps Down," KPCC, November 20, 2009.

Howard Blume, "Green Dot Charter Schools Founder Repays Group $50,866," *Los Angeles Times*, December 2, 2009.

Alexander Russo, "Extreme School Makeover," *Miller-McCune*, March 16, 2010.

Chapter 20: Turnaround Fever

Alexander Russo, "Green Dot Founder Reported Leaving," *This Week in Education*, November 21, 2009. Retrieved from http://www.thisweekineducation.com.

Bruce Fuller, "Palace Revolt in Los Angeles?" *Education Next*, Summer, 2010.

Epilogue

Sam Dillon, "Cost of Progress at a Failing School," *New York Times*, June 24, 2010.

Howard Blume, "Annual Test Scores Rise in L.A. Unified Schools," *Los Angeles Times*, August 17, 2010.

"Lessons from Locke," *Los Angeles Times*, August 20, 2010.

Jay Mathews, "What Jerry Bracey Would Have Said About Locke High," *Washington Post*, October 12, 2010.

About the Author

Alexander Russo is a freelance education writer and blogger whose reporting and commentary have appeared in *The Washington Post*, *Slate*, *Washington Monthly*, *Miller-McCune*, and several other publications. He is the author of education blogs *This Week In Education*, *District 299*, and *Hot For Education*. He holds a master's degree from the Harvard Graduate School of Education and a bachelor's degree from Stanford. He taught at the Harvard School (now Harvard-Westlake) in Los Angeles and was a researcher at Policy Studies Associates in Washington, D.C. He advised U.S. Senator Dianne Feinstein on education issues during the first Clinton administration and worked for U.S. Senator Jeff Bingaman during much of the second. He also worked as a special assistant to New York City Schools Chancellor Ramon Cortines. He was a Spencer Education Journalism Fellow at the Columbia Graduate School of Journalism in 2008–2009. Born in London and raised in Chicago, he currently lives in Brooklyn, N.Y.

Index